T0235927

Lecture Notes in Computer Science 14552

Founding Editors

Gerhard Goos
Juris Hartmanis

Editorial Board Members

The series Lecture Notes in Computer Science (LNCS), including its subseries Lecture Notes in Artificial Intelligence (LNAI) and Lecture Notes in Bioinformatics (LNBI), has established itself as a medium for the publication of new developments in computer science and information technology research, teaching, and education.

LNCS enjoys close cooperation with the computer science R & D community, the series counts many renowned academics among its volume editors and paper authors, and collaborates with prestigious societies. Its mission is to serve this international community by providing an invaluable service, mainly focused on the publication of conference and workshop proceedings and postproceedings. LNCS commenced publication in 1973.

Mohamed Mosbah · Florence Sèdes ·
Nadia Tawbi · Toufik Ahmed ·
Nora Boulahia-Cuppens · Joaquin Garcia-Alfaro
Editors

Foundations and Practice of Security

16th International Symposium, FPS 2023
Bordeaux, France, December 11–13, 2023
Revised Selected Papers, Part II

 Springer

Editors
Mohamed Mosbah 🆔
University of Bordeaux
Bordeaux, France

Florence Sèdes 🆔
Toulouse III - Paul Sabatier University
Toulouse, France

Nadia Tawbi 🆔
Université Laval
Québec, QC, Canada

Toufik Ahmed 🆔
University of Bordeaux
Bordeaux, France

Nora Boulahia-Cuppens 🆔
Polytechnique Montréal
Montreal, QC, Canada

Joaquin Garcia-Alfaro 🆔
Telecom SudParis
Palaiseau, France

ISSN 0302-9743   ISSN 1611-3349 (electronic)
Lecture Notes in Computer Science
ISBN 978-3-031-57539-6   ISBN 978-3-031-57540-2 (eBook)
https://doi.org/10.1007/978-3-031-57540-2

This Springer imprint is published by the registered company Springer Nature Switzerland AG
The registered company address is: Gewerbestrasse 11, 6330 Cham, Switzerland

Paper in this product is recyclable.

Foreword Message from the Chairs

The 16th International Symposium on Foundations and Practice of Security (FPS 2023) was hosted by the Bordeaux Institute of Technology (Bordeaux INP), in Bordeaux, France, from December 11 to December 13, 2023.

FPS's aim was to discuss and exchange theoretical and practical ideas that address security issues in interconnected systems. It allowed scientists to present their work and establish links and promote scientific collaboration, joint research programs, and student exchanges between institutions involved in this important and fast-moving research field.

The call for papers welcomed submissions spanning the full range of theoretical and applied work including user research, methods, tools, simulations, demos, and practical evaluations. We also invited researchers and practitioners working in privacy, security, resiliency, trustworthy data systems, and related areas to submit their original papers. This year, special care was given to enhancing Cybersecurity and Resiliency with Artificial Intelligence.

FPS 2023 received 80 submissions from countries all over the world. On average, each paper was reviewed (single blind) by three program committee members, and there were several online discussions in case of divergent evaluations. The Program Committee selected 27 regular papers and 8 short papers for presentation. An invited paper was also selected for publication in this book. The selected papers have been organized in the following sections: Artificial Intelligence and Cybersecurity; Security Analysis; Phishing and Social Networks; Vulnerabilities, Exploits and Threats; Malware Analysis; Security Design and Short Papers.

December 2023

Nadia Tawbi
Florence Sèdes
Mohamed Mosbah
Nora Boulahia-Cuppens
Toufik Ahmed

Organization

General Chairs

Toufik Ahmed — Bordeaux INP, France
Nora Cuppens — École Polytechnique de Montréal, Canada

Program Committee Chairs

Mohamed Mosbah — Bordeaux INP, France
Florence Sèdes — Université Toulouse III Paul Sabatier, France
Nadia Tawbi — Université Laval, Canada

Keynote Chair

Guy-Vincent Jourdan — University of Ottawa, Canada

Local Organization Chair

Léo Mendiboure — Université Gustave Eiffel, France

Publications Chair

Joaquin Garcia-Alfaro — Institut Polytechnique de Paris, France

Publicity Chairs

Raphaël Khoury — Université du Québec en Outaouais, Canada
Paria Shirani — University of Ottawa, Canada
Reda Yaich — IRT SystemX, France

Program Committee

Carlisle Adams	University of Ottawa, Canada
Esma Aïmeur	Université de Montréal, Canada
Furkan Alaca	Queen's University, Canada
Abdelmalek Benzekri	Université Toulouse 3 Paul Sabatier, France
Anis Bkakria	IRT SystemX, France
Guillaume Bonfante	LORIA – Université de Lorraine, France
Ana Rosa Cavalli	Institut Polytechnique de Paris, France
Xihui Chen	University of Luxembourg, Luxembourg
Kimberly A. Cornell	University at Albany, USA
Frédéric Cuppens	Polytechnique Montréal, Canada
Nora Cuppens-Boulahia	Polytechnique Montréal, Canada
Xavier de Carné de Carnavalet	Hong Kong Polytechnic University, China
Benoit Dupont	Université de Montréal, Canada
Latifa El Bargui	University of Ottawa, Canada
Sebastien Gambs	Université du Québec à Montréal, Canada
Joaquin Garcia-Alfaro	Institut Polytechnique de Paris, France
Talal Halabi	Université Laval, Canada
Sylvain Hallé	Université du Québec à Chicoutimi, Canada
Abdessamad Imine	LORIA-Inria Lorraine, France
Jason Jaskolka	Carleton University, Canada
Mathieu Jaume	Sorbonne Université, France
Houda Jmila	Commissariat à l'Energie Atomique, France
Guy-Vincent Jourdan	University of Ottawa, Canada
Raphaël Khoury	Université du Québec en Outaouais, Canada
Hyoungshick Kim	Sungkyunkwan University, South Korea
Hyungjoon Koo	Sungkyunkwan University, South Korea
Evangelos Kranakis	Carleton University, Canada
Romain Laborde	University Paul Sabatier Toulouse III, France
Pascal Lafourcade	University Clermont Auvergne, France
Maryline Laurent	Institut Polytechnique de Paris, France
Mounier Laurent	Laboratoire Vérimag, France
Olivier Levillain	Institut Polytechnique de Paris, France
Luigi Logrippo	Université du Québec en Outaouais, Canada
Taous Madi	King Abdullah University of Science and Technology, Saudi Arabia
Jean-Yves Marion	Université de Lorraine, France
Andrew M. Marshall	University of Mary Washington, USA
Daiki Miyahara	University of Electro-Communications, Japan
Mohamed Mosbah	LaBRI – University of Bordeaux, France
Djedjiga Mouheb	University of Sharjah, United Arab Emirates

Paliath Narendran	University at Albany, USA
Omer Landry Nguena Timo	Université du Québec en Outaouais, Canada
Marie-Laure Potet	Laboratoire Vérimag, France
Isabel Praça	Instituto Superior de Engenharia do Porto, Portugal
Silvio Ranise	University of Trento and Fondazione Bruno Kessler, Italy
Jean-Marc Robert	École de technologie supérieure, Canada
Michael Rusinowitch	LORIA – Inria Nancy, France
Kazuo Sakiyama	University of Electro-Communications, Japan
Khosro Salmani	Mount Royal University, Canada
Giada Sciarretta	Fondazione Bruno Kessler, Italy
Florence Sèdes	Université Toulouse III Paul Sabatier, France
Paria Shirani	University of Ottawa, Canada
Renaud Sirdey	Commissariat à l'Energie Atomique, France
Natalia Stakhanova	University of Saskatchewan, Canada
Nadia Tawbi	Université Laval, Canada
Sadegh Torabi	Concordia University, Canada
Jun Yan	Concordia University, Canada
Nicola Zannone	Eindhoven University of Technology, The Netherlands

Steering Committee

Frédéric Cuppens	École Polytechnique de Montréal, Canada
Nora Cuppens-Boulahia	École Polytechnique de Montréal, Canada
Mourad Debbabi	University of Concordia, Canada
Joaquin Garcia-Alfaro	Institut Polytechnique de Paris, France
Evangelos Kranakis	Carleton University, Canada
Pascal Lafourcade	University of Clermont Auvergne, France
Jean-Yves Marion	Mines de Nancy, France
Ali Miri	Toronto Metropolitan University, Canada
Rei Safavi-Naini	Calgary University, Canada
Nadia Tawbi	Université Laval, Canada

Additional Reviewers

Shashank Arora	Guillaume Gagnon
Pradeep K. Atrey	Asmaa Hailane
Stefano Berlato	Frédéric Hayek
Josee Desharnais	Li Huang

Padmavathi Iyer
Nerys Jimenez-Pichardo
Mohamed Ali Kandi
Youcef Korichi
Vinh Hoa La
Abir Laraba
Wissam Mallouli
Gael Marcadet
Majid Mollaeefar

Manh-Dung Nguyen
Huu Nghia Nguyen
Charles Olivier-Anclin
Sankita Patel
Josue Ruiz
Amir Sharif
Valeria Valdés
Badreddine Yacine Yacheur
Atefeh Zareh Chahoki

Formal Verification of Security Protocols: the Squirrel Prover (Keynote)

Stéphanie Delaune

Univ Rennes, CNRS, IRISA, France

Abstract. Security protocols are widely used today to secure transactions that take place through public channels like the Internet. Common applications involve the secure transfer of sensitive information like credit card numbers or user authentication on a system. Because of their increasing ubiquity in many important applications (e.g. electronic commerce, government-issued ID), a very important research challenge consists in developing methods and verification tools to increase our trust on security protocols, and so on the applications that rely on them.

Formal methods have introduced various approaches to prove that security protocols indeed guarantee the expected security properties. Tools like ProVerif [5] and Tamarin [6] analyse protocols in the symbolic model, leveraging techniques from model-checking, automated reasoning, and concurrency theory. However, it's essential to note that security in the symbolic model doesn't necessarily imply security in the cryptographer's standard model—the computational model—where attackers operate as probabilistic polynomial time Turing machines. Verification techniques for the computational model, though crucial, often exhibit less flexibility or automation compared to tools in the symbolic model.

In recent collaborative efforts, my colleagues and I have proposed a novel approach [1], building upon the Computationally Complete Symbolic Attacker (CCSA) logic introduced by Gergei Bana and Hubert Comon a few years ago [3, 4]. This approach has been implemented in a new proof assistant called SQUIRREL, and the effectiveness of the SQUIRREL prover has been validated across various case studies. The SQUIRREL tool, a user-friendly manual, as well as an online platform to experiment SQUIRREL without installing it, are now available: https://squirrel-prover.github.io.

This work received funding from the France 2030 program managed by the French National Research Agency under grant agreement No. ANR-22-PECY-0006.

Figure 1 shows a screenshot of the SQUIRREL prover. On the left, a description of the Basic Hash protocol written in the input language of SQUIRREL is depicted. The scenario under study features several reader sessions with access to a database, and several tags where each tag can play multiple sessions. The exists instruction encodes the database lookup performed by the reader.

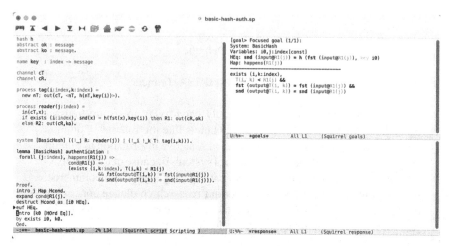

Fig. 1.   Screenshot of the SQUIRREL prover on the Basic Hash protocol.

Then, an authentication property on the Basic Hash protocol is expressed. Here cond@R1(j) is a macro which stands for the condition of action R1(j) – the condition for executing the then branch of the reader. The authentication lemma expresses that, whenever this condition holds, there must be some session k of tag i (the one using key(i)) that has been executed before R1(j). Moreover, the output of the tag's action should coincide with the input of the reader's action. Finally, this authentication goal is proved using a succession of six tactics.

On the right, the status of the proof after the execution of the three first tactics is shown. The hypotheses are written above the horizontal line, and the goal that remains to be proved is written below the horizontal line. At this stage of the proof, we can see that some hypotheses have been introduced (intro tactic), and the macro cond@R1(j) has been expanded (expand tactic). The next step of the proof consists of applying the euf tactic (unforgeability of h). Roughly, if snd(input@R1(j)) is a valid hash of fst(input@R1(j)), thus the term fst(input@R1(j)) must be equal to a message that has previously been hashed. As the only application of the h function is in the action performed by the tag and is applied on the nonce nT, after applying the euf tactic, we obtain:

```
[goal> Focused goal (1/1):
System: BasicHash
Variables: i0,j:index[const]
HEq: snd (input@R1(j)) = h (fst (input@R1(j)), key i0)
Hap: happens(R1(j))
--------------------------------------------------
(exists (k:index), T(i0, k) < R1(j) && fst (input@R1(j)) = nT (i0, k)) =>
exists (i,k:index),
   T(i, k) < R1(j) &&
   fst (output@T(i, k)) = fst (input@R1(j)) &&
   snd (output@T(i, k)) = snd (input@R1(j))
```

In Fig. 2, some results that have been obtained with the SQUIRREL prover are summarised. The number of LoC mentioned includes both the model and the proof script. The cryptographic assumptions on which the proof relies on are also indicated, as well as the security properties under study.

Protocol name	LoC	Assumptions	Security Properties
Basic Hash	100	PRF, EUF	authentication & unlinkability
Hash Lock	130	PRF, EUF	authentication & unlinkability
LAK (with pairs)	250	PRF, EUF	authentication & unlinkability
MW	300	PRF, EUF, XOR	authentication & unlinkability
Feldhofer	270	ENC-KP, INT-CTXT	authentication & unlinkability
Private authentication	100	CCA₁, ENC-KP	anonymity
Signed DDH [ISO 9798-3]	240	EUF, DDH	authentication & strong secrecy
CANAuth	450	EUF	authentication
SLK06	80	EUF	authentication
YPLRK05	160	EUF	authentication

Fig. 2. Some results obtained with the SQUIRREL prover on various protocols [1, 2].

References

1. Baelde, D., Delaune, S., Jacomme, C., Koutsos, A., Moreau, S.: An interactive prover for protocol verification in the computational model. In: Proceedings of the 42nd IEEE Symposium on Security and Privacy (S&P'21), San Fransisco/Virtual, USA (May 2021)
2. Baelde, D., Delaune, S., Koutsos, A., Moreau, S.: Cracking the stateful nut: computational proofs of stateful security protocols using the SQUIRREL proof assistant. In: Proceedings of the 35th IEEE Computer Security Foundations Symposium (CSF'22), pp. 289–304, Haifa, Israel. IEEE Computer Society Press (Aug 2022)
3. Bana, G., Comon-Lundh, H.: Towards unconditional soundness: computationally complete symbolic attacker. In: Degano, P., Guttman, J.D. (eds.) Principles of Security and Trust. POST 2012. Lecture Notes in Computer Science, vol. 7215, pp. 189–208. Springer, Berlin (2012). https://doi.org/10.1007/978-3-642-28641-4_11
4. Bana, G., Comon-Lundh, H.: A computationally complete symbolic attacker for equivalence properties. In Proceedings of the 21st Conference on Computer and Communications Security (CCS'14), pp. 609–620. ACM (2014)

5. Blanchet, B.: An efficient cryptographic protocol verifier based on prolog rules. In: Proceedings of the 14th IEEE Computer Security Foundations Workshop (CSFW'01), pp. 82–96. IEEE Computer Society (2001)
6. Meier, S., Schmidt, B., Cremers, C., Basin, D.: The TAMARIN prover for the symbolic analysis of security protocols. In: Sharygina, N., Veith, H. (eds.) Computer Aided Verification. CAV 2013. Lecture Notes in Computer Science, vol. 8044, pp. 696–701. Springer, Berlin (2013). https://doi.org/10.1007/978-3-642-39799-8_48

Contents – Part II

Contents – Part I

Phishing and Social Network

Vulnerabilities and Exploits

Network and System Threat

Malware Analysis

Security Design

Short Papers

UCAT: The Uniform Categorization for Access Control

Denis Obrezkov[1]([⊠])[ID] and Karsten Sohr[2][ID]

[1] TIB Leibniz Information Centre for Science and Technology, Hannover, Germany
denis.obrezkov@tib.eu
[2] University of Bremen, Bremen, Germany
sohr@tzi.de

Abstract. The basic primitives of access control models evolve together with the development of new technologies. The increased availability of computers in organizations brought the notion of roles in, the growing popularity of online social networks led to access control models based on relationships. The new era introduces new challenges. One of those is related to data management in collaborative platforms. Being involved in numerous collaborations, the users need convenient solutions to express their access control preferences. In this paper we address this problem by developing an access control model based on categorization. Relying on evidence from cognitive science, we employ categories as a natural primitive for expressing users' access control preferences. We develop our model using a fragment of hybrid logic and evaluate its performance in a simulated environment.

1 Introduction

The evolution of access control models follows the development of technology. Earlier access control models, like Bell-LaPadula [4] or lattice-based [11], operated primarily on subjects, objects, information flows, actions—keeping a high level of generalization. The increased availability of computer systems for organizations led to the appearance of such models as Role-Based Access Control (RBAC) [13]. The latter leveraged notions of roles and users, thereby closing a gap between the model and the target domain. Lastly, the widespread use of personal technology and the Internet gave a birth to user-centric models. For instance, Relationship-Based Access Control (ReBAC) systems allow a user to specify a local policy based on their relationships with others [6].

The modern era brings new challenges. Collaborative platforms require policies that would allow users to specify their access control preferences not only with regard to other users but also with regard to data [17]. The data itself is starting to play a more prominent role in new systems. For instance, in the scientific domain the importance of data-centricity is reflected in FAIR data management principles. FAIR is defined as a set of guidelines: data should be Findable, Accessible, Interoperable, and Reusable [19]. The aim of the guidelines is to empower researchers with more rigorous management of scientific digital

M. Mosbah et al. (Eds.): FPS 2023, LNCS 14552, pp. 3–14, 2024.
https://doi.org/10.1007/978-3-031-57540-2_1

objects. In the context of access control, it is interesting to consider the Accessibility principle. Among other points, it is stated that "the protocol allows for an authentication and authorization procedure, where necessary". The authorization procedure itself, however, is out of scope of the guidelines.

The problem of data- and user-centric permission management is a prominent challenge for collaborative platforms [17,18]. Classic access control policies might not fit well the new environment. In the context of scholarly publishing platform, one can consider a situation when a researcher shares their digital manuscript draft with their colleagues from other institutions, with a third-party proofreader, and with a reviewer. It would be very notorious to establish the appropriate roles in an RBAC-system: the reviewer and the colleagues might have similar roles in the system. Additionally, after the positive review, it might be desired to grant the access to a broader audience, changing the type of the document from "draft" to "accepted paper". In that case, classical ReBAC models are also out of consideration, since they do not account for object types.

In a modern collaborative system we should allow a user to express their preferences towards resources and other people. One of the approaches is to account for the main mechanics behind access control—categorization. In case of ReBAC, a user categorizes requesters, e.g. as friends or colleagues. In the Bell-LaPadula model, an authority assigns sensitivity labels to files (for instance, "secret", "top secret"), thereby categorizing them. Given that cognitive science considers categorization to be the basic mechanism behind the perception of both objects [12] and people [2], it seems desirable to develop a model that would combine a user-centered view of ReBAC models with a uniform and deliberate application of categorization.

In this paper, we propose a user-centric model that accounts for both types of relationships: with subject (people, applications) and objects (data resources, files). In the next section, we review some established ways of dealing with categories and relations in access control. In Sect. 3 we introduce hybrid logic, the formalism that we base our model on. In Sect. 4, we describe our model. Subsequently, in Sect. 5 we show examples of how our model can be used from both user- and platform- centric perspectives, and in Sect. 6 we evaluate the performance of our model in an artificial collaborative environment. Lastly, in Sect. 7 we discuss the implications of our contribution and the interesting directions for future work.

2   Related Work

In this section, we review some of the prominent approaches in access control. We selected these works since they represent different ways of accounting for relationships between subjects and objects.

The need to reflect an organizational structure in a company's data access policies led to the appearance of the Role-Based Access Control model, or RBAC [13]. RBAC allows an organization to establish a mapping between a role of an employee and a set of desired permissions. Thereby, for instance, an *accountant* might be allowed to access only financial reports, while a *developer* might be granted access to code repositories.

Social networks brought new challenges to the field. Fong proposed to consider users' relationships as a basis for access control decisions [14]. The author leverages modal logic as a basis for his policy language. Using modal operators of necessity ($[i]$) and possibility ($<i>$), he allows such formulas as: $\langle spouse \rangle$a ("grant access to the owner's spouse."), and $\langle -parent \rangle$a $\wedge$ $[-parent]$a ("grant access if accessor is the only child of the owner"). Although this formalism accounts for interpersonal relationships, it still lacks a personal aspect: it is hard to make a decision from a certain user's perspective.

To address the limitations of the previously introduced modal logic in access control, Bruns et al. proposed to leverage hybrid logic [6]. Hybrid logic can be viewed as an extension of modal logic with enumerated graph nodes (see Sect. 3 for more details). It allows one to evaluate formulas from a certain point of view. To achieve this, two operators are introduced: $@_i$ and $\downarrow x$. The first operator jumps to a node, named by i. The second, binding operator, binds the current node to the variable x. In their approach, the authors propose to evaluate formulas of a type $@_{own}\phi \wedge @_{req}\psi$. Thereby, the policy is evaluated from two perspectives: one of the owner and one of the requester. The safety problem is considered in the view of local model checking. It should be noted that the proposed system has a strong flavor of user-centricity, even though it is a formal access control model.

The need to account for user-object relations is partially addressed in the work by Damen et al. [10]. The authors introduce CollAC, the framework that extends the aforementioned work of Bruns et al. It is proposed to use a notion of archetype that accounts for the relations between users and files. The authors avoid the inclusion of files or objects into the access control model. Instead, they define additional roles for users, such as Data Host or Data Provider. These roles are introduced as free variables. In our view, this solution might lack flexibility in scenarios where a large amount of relationship types exist between users and objects.

The work of Crampton and Sellwood introduces a new framework based on path conditions [9]. The latter are defined as chains of relationships that make it possible to identify, whether a particular principal is associated with a request. The authors also propose to use a two-step approach: first, to determine relevant principals, second, to look for a corresponding authorization policy for the matched principals. Unlike classical ReBAC model, the proposed framework supports general-purpose computing systems. At the same time, the path conditions are similar to models, based on modal logic: the latter do not provide local operators, such as $@_n$, for expressing policies that account for a certain viewpoint.

The idea of considering object-to-object relations is realized in several frameworks. Carminati et al. propose to use semantic technologies for access control [7,8]. The authors utilize modeling languages to encode security rules, they also employ reasoners to inference new relationships between entities. Ahmed et al. introduces OOReBAC, a framework that accounts for object-to-object relationships [1]. It should be noted that OOReBAC misses some important features of ReBAC, for instance, it considers only symmetric relationships. Thereby, it is not possible to account for a specific user's perspective (e.g. "Alice thinks that Bob is her friend, Bob considers Alice to be an acquaintance").

The presented works reveal several desirable features. First, there is a need for a flexible model that would be able to account for the underlying structure of an organization or community. Second, it is possible to consider different relationships in the model: user-to-object, user-to-user, object-to-object. Last, it might be desirable to have an ability of reasoning from a certain user perspective, thereby making access control user-centric.

3   Hybrid Logic

The need to account for different types of relationships together with a desired ability to incorporate user-centric perspectives shapes our requirements for the underlying mathematical foundation. It is not sufficient for us to rely on the apparatus of modal or description logic as done in the earlier-mentioned works (i.e. [7,14]). These systems do not provide easy solutions for making policies, accounting for a certain viewpoint. For similar reasons, we cannot employ the framework of path conditions, as in [9]. Given this, we base our framework on hybrid logic [5]. The latter is shown to be useful for accounting for a certain user's preferences [6,10].

Informally speaking, a model based on hybrid logic can be viewed as a graph. The nodes of the graph represent entities, with the edges reflecting relations between them. Hybrid logic allows one to build formulas using modalities of necessity and possibility. The intuition behind these two terms is the following. Let us consider a node w, connected with zero or more nodes via relation r. We say that $\langle r \rangle \phi$ ('possibly ϕ via r') is true at w, if ϕ is true at some nodes accessible via relation r from w. We say that $[r]\phi$ ('necessarily ϕ via r'), if ϕ is true at all nodes accessible vie relation r from w. Thereby, the meanings of necessity and possibility are similar to those in modal logic. In addition to the modalities, hybrid logic introduces the mechanism of nodes enumeration. In this case each node is assigned a unique name, thereby, one can refer to a specific node in a formula. To achieve this, two operators are introduced: @ and $\downarrow$. The first one, $@_s$ ('at s') shifts the evaluation point to the node, named s. The binding operator $\downarrow x$ allows us to bind variable x to the current point of evaluation, thereby, enabling us to refer to the current point later in the formula.

Definition 1. *Given the set NOM of nominal symbols, the set REL of relational symbols, the set VAR of propositional symbols, and the set VAR of variables, we can define a well-formed formula of the hybrid language HL(@, $\downarrow$) using the following recursive definition:*

$$\phi ::= top \mid p \mid s \mid \neg\phi \mid \phi_1 \wedge \phi_2 \mid \langle r \rangle \phi \mid \langle -r \rangle \phi \mid @_s\phi \mid \downarrow x\phi$$

where $p \in PROP$, $s \in NOM \cup VAR$, $x \in VAR$, $r \in REL$, and ϕ_1, ϕ_2 are formulas.

Definition 2. *A hybrid model M is defined as a triple $M = (W, \Omega, V)$, where W is a non-empty set of nodes, $\Omega(r)$ is a binary relation on W for all $r \in R$, and V is a total function, such that $V : PROP \cup NOM \to 2^W$, and $V(n)$ is a singleton for all $n \in NOM$. The satisfaction relation for $M, w, g \models \phi$ is defined in Fig. 1.*

$$M, w, g \models \top \quad\quad \text{always}$$
$$M, w, g \models x \quad \text{iff} \quad w = g(x)$$
$$M, w, g \models n \quad \text{iff} \quad V(n) = w$$
$$M, w, g \models p \quad \text{iff} \quad w \in V(p)$$
$$M, w, g \models \neg\phi \quad \text{iff} \quad M, w, g \not\models \phi$$
$$M, w, g \models \phi_1 \wedge \phi_2 \quad \text{iff} \quad M, w, g \models \phi_1 \text{ and } M, w, g \models \phi_2$$
$$M, w, g \models \langle r \rangle \phi \quad \text{iff} \quad M, w', g \models \phi \text{ for some } (w, w') \in \Omega(r)$$
$$M, w, g \models \langle -r \rangle \phi \quad \text{iff} \quad M, w', g \models \phi \text{ for some } (w', w) \in \Omega(r)$$
$$M, w, g \models @_n \phi \quad \text{iff} \quad M, w^*, g \models \phi \text{ where } V(n) = w^*$$
$$M, w, g \models @_x \phi \quad \text{iff} \quad M, g(x), g \models \phi$$
$$M, w, g \models \downarrow x \phi \quad \text{iff} \quad M, w, g[x \mapsto w] \models \phi$$

Fig. 1. Definition of satisfaction relation $M, w, g \models \phi$. The formula ϕ of hybrid logic HL is true in node w of model M under valuation g.

The intuition behind the model is the following. The function $V(p)$ maps a propositional symbol to the set of nodes where the latter is true. For a nominal symbol it returns a node, to which this nominal is assigned. As we discussed earlier, hybrid logic allows a user to enumerate nodes, thereby $V(n)$ maps a nominal to a node, 'named' by this nominal. Lastly, the valuation function g is a mapping from variables to nodes.

4   UCAT: Uniform Categorization for Access Control

The traditional ReBAC model accounts only for the viewpoints of an object owner and a requester. In other words, a policy is based on how the owner 'treats' the requester. Given the evidence from cognitive science that people apply categorization to both persons and objects [2,12], it seems natural to include 'relationships' to objects into the decision making as well. In our model we enable users to specify how they categorize other users and their own objects and to create policies based on these categories. Thereby, the following statement becomes possible: "grant access to my *private* files to my *family* members." In line with our main principle, we call our access control model Uniform Categorization, or UCAT.

Definition 3. *Let* HL(own,req,dobj) *be the set of formulas of* HL, *where:*

- own,req,dobj *are the only free variables,*
- *formulas are built using Boolean combinations of formulas of the form* $@_{own}$, $@_{req}$, *and* $@_{dobj}$.

Similar to the work of Bruns et al. [6] we refer to formulas of HL(own,req,dobj) as policies. Given $\circ = \{\wedge, \vee\}$, general policy pattern has the following form:

$$@_{own}\phi_1 \circ @_{req}\phi_2 \circ @_{dobj}\phi_3$$

The leftmost part $@_{own}\phi_1$ specifies a viewpoint of a resource owner. The middle statement $@_{req}\phi_2$ represents a perspective of a requester. The rightmost part of the formula allows one to make policies that account for relationships between objects. That might be useful when objects' interconnections can be utilized for security decisions. For example, it is natural to grant access to a document and also to new versions of the document. In other words, the relationship 'new-version' might be used in an access control policy.

Authorization Decisions. Each access requests is evaluated according to the following rule. Given a model M, a data object d in *Obj*, an object owner o, an access requester r, and a corresponding formula *pol*, the following condition should hold:

$$M, [own \mapsto o, req \mapsto r, dobj \mapsto d] \models pol \tag{1}$$

This statement binds free variables own, req, dobj to an object owner, a requester, a requested object and then evaluates the formula *pol*. Thereby, each authorization decision is done be evaluating a respective formula. For the evaluation one can use a local model-checking algorithm provided in the ReBAC paper [6]. The only change required for the algorithm is to include the variable dobj into the procedure of free variable binding.

5 Use Cases

In this section we demonstrate the applicability of our model from three different perspectives. First, we demonstrate how a user can specify their policies, considering their categorization of files and other people. Second, we provide examples, representing a traditional single authority use-case. Lastly, we demonstrate policies, adopting a data-centric perspective.

Example 1. A User-Centric Perspective. In the user-centric scenario a Bob wants to allow his colleagues to access his paper drafts. As it is shown in Fig. 2a, Bob has already described Alice as a colleague, Eve as a competitor, and a certain paper as a draft. The possible policy to achieve Bob's goal is $@_{own}\langle colleague\rangle$req. It can be translated as "a requester should be accessible via 'colleague' relation". Similar to ReBAC, policies are associated with objects. UCAT, however, allows one to specify policies of higher granularity. Consider this formula: $@_{own}\langle colleague\rangle$req $\wedge$ $@_{own}\langle draft\rangle$dobj. This policy allows Bob to

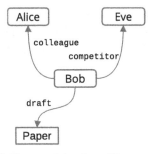 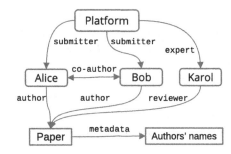

(a) User-centric view. The graph represents how Bob categorizes Alice and Eve, and his paper

(b) Platform-centric view. Platform assigns roles to its users and to their relations with uploaded documents and other users.

Fig. 2. Two versions of an access control graph.

state that access is granted to all his colleagues to files that he considers as drafts. Together with attaching a policy to an object, UCAT leverages the hybrid model binding mechanism to map an object to the free variable dobj.

Example 2. A Single Authority Perspective. Our platform-centric view represents a traditional model with a single authority (see Fig. 2b). It is interesting to note that this use case is just a variation of the previous one: Platform can be treated as a common user. Several rules can be demonstrated. For instance, let us consider a use case of a scientific publishing system. It is desirable for a platform to allow authors to access metadata of their papers. There are at least two ways to achieve this goal. First, it is possible to make a policy from a requester's point of view: $@_{req}\langle author\rangle\langle metadata\rangle$dobj. With this formula we state that the requester should be an author of something that is related with the 'metadata' relation to the object. To allow experts of the platform to access any paper, we can specify the following policy: $@_{own}\langle expert\rangle$req. Since we employ a single-authority perspective, the own variable is bound to 'Platform' (e.g. to a platform's administrator). Thereby the last policy can be interpreted as "grant access to those experts, who are considered experts by the platform".

The user-centric and platform-centric perspectives can be effectively combined. A platform might have default relations to its users, e.g. categorizing them as submitters or experts. The system can automatically assign the 'co-author' label to the relation between authors of one paper. A default platform-wide policy might allow co-authors to see all the available works of each other. On top of that, a single user can assign their own labels to their co-authors for a more fine-grained access control. The latter might be required if the user involved in several projects with conflicts of interest among co-authors.

Example 3. A Data-Centric Perspective. In addition to user- and platform-centric views, our model allows for shifting the decision-evaluation point to an object. For instance, we can reformulate a policy that allows authors to access their data: $@_{dobj}\langle -author\rangle$req. In that case access is granted, if the requested object is connected with a reverse *author* relation with the requester.

We can also consider relations between objects. For example, to grant access to the paper's metadata to the paper's authors, we can construct the following policy: $@_{\text{dobj}}\langle -metadata\rangle\langle -author\rangle\texttt{req}$. It is also possible to grant access to papers with any metadata: $@_{\text{dobj}}\langle metadata\rangle\top$. Object-to-objects permissions are specifically useful when objects have some explicit relation, for instance, representing different versions of a single document.

6   Performance Evaluation

In order to assess the feasibility of our model, we performed an evaluation of several policies. We constructed an artificial environment that resembles a platform for a scientific publishing system. The system exhibits the following structure (see Fig. 2b). Users can be registered as submitters or experts; they might be related with a 'co-author' relation. Some users are authors of papers, and some are reviewers. Each paper is related to its authors' names with the 'metadata' relation.

The construction of the graph, representing the aforementioned system, included the following steps. First, we leveraged the Arxiv General Relativity and Quantum Cosmology (GR-QC) collaboration network dataset from the SNAP project [16]. The dataset describes co-authorship relationships based on e-print arXiv papers in the GR-QC category. In our graph we included these relations from the dataset by specifying symmetric edge with a 'co-author' label. Second, we introduced an artificial node 'Platform' and connected it to all author nodes, randomly assigning the edges either 'submitter' or 'expert' labels. Third, to each submitter we attached 10 papers, connecting them with an 'author'-labeled edge. For each paper we randomly chose one additional author (among the co-authors of the original author) and two reviewers, randomly choosing them among experts. Lastly, each paper was associated with a node, representing its authors' names. The edges between these two types of nodes were assigned 'metadata' labels. The constructed graph aims to represent a use-case scenario of a scientific event with proceedings.

We evaluated the following policies:

$$@_{\text{own}}\langle\text{co-author}\rangle\texttt{req} \tag{Policy 1}$$

$$@_{\text{req}}\langle\text{author}\rangle\texttt{dobj} \lor @_{\text{own}}\langle\text{expert}\rangle\texttt{req} \tag{Policy 2}$$

$$@_{\text{dobj}}\langle\text{-metadata}\rangle\langle\text{-author}\rangle\langle\text{co-author}\rangle\texttt{req} \tag{Policy 3}$$

$$@_{\text{req}}\langle\text{co-author}\rangle\texttt{own} \lor @_{\text{own}}\langle\text{-submitter}\rangle\langle\text{expert}\rangle\texttt{req} \tag{Policy 4}$$

The first formula represents the policy that allows a requester to access an object, if they are related to the owner with the 'co-author' relation. In other words, to obtain access, a requester should be categorized as a co-author by the file owner. The second policy grants access to either authors of the object, or to the experts on the platform. The third formula aims to restrict access to authors' names. In that case access is granted only to those requesters, who are co-authors of the authors of the paper. The last policy states that a requester should be a co-author of an object's owner, or she should be an expert. To evaluate each policy we implemented an adopted version of the Local Model Checking algorithm for the ReBAC's Hybrid Model [6]. Our implementation does not significantly affect the complexity of policy evaluation, since it only adds one free variable (to account for relationships with objects). In our implementation we perform simple recursive descent parsing of the given policies. In *Policy 1* and *Policy 4* the free variable own is bound to a random user (a user-centric perspective), while in *Policy 2* it is bound to Platform node (a single authority perspective).

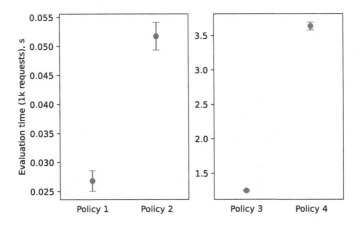

Fig. 3. Evaluation of four access control policies. Each policy was evaluated 1000 times. The experiment was repeated 10 times, the means and 95% confidence intervals are presented.

We performed the evaluation using commodity hardware with the following configuration: AMD Ryzen 7 5700G, 3.8 GHz processor, 32 GB RAM (DDR4, 3200 MHz), WD SN350 NVMe SSD. The computer was running Ubuntu 22.04 operating system with Linux 5.15 kernel. To create our simulated environment we leveraged Python 3.10.12 together with networkx 3.1 library. The latter allows one to create and process graph-based networks [15].

The evaluation results are shown in Fig. 3. The first and the second policies were evaluated in less than 60 ms, while for more complex policies it took less than 4 s to be evaluated (1000 requests were made). The observed difference can be explained by the structure of the policies. *Policy 1* and *Policy 2* involve only a search of depth of 1 relation. *Policy 3* and *Policy 4* required a search of depth of 2 relations (the 'metadata' relation in *Policy 3* is a one-to-one relation, not significantly affecting the results). Given that many real-life scenarios only involve relation paths of length 1 (a user tags objects and not between-object relations, a company assigns sensitivity labels to employees), we believe that our framework could be a good solution in many practical applications.

7   Discussion

Our work can be viewed as an extension of the existing access control models. To achieve user-centricity, we base our model on hybrid logic. The latter allows one to evaluate access requests from a certain user perspective. Additionally, we explicitly rely on categorization, since it is shown to be the basic cognitive mechanism of human reasoning about other people and objects. In the next paragraphs we provide an overview of how our proposition is related to other prominent research models.

The UCAT model can be used to represent simple RBAC policies. One of the core ideas behind RBAC is that an organization assigns roles to users. In UCAT terms, the organization is the owner of the files and it categorizes its employees. For instance, a role 'manager' in an RBAC system can be represented via relation $@_{own}\langle manager \rangle$. In a similar fashion it is possible to account for the relationships between permissions and allowed actions (for instance, via binding a free variable dobj to the requested action). Additionally, UCAT allows one to specify local policies. For example, a global policy might assign Bob to the 'manager' role and authorize other managers to access his files. Bob can additionally label some of his colleagues as 'competitors' and deny them access to 'in-progress' files. Apparently, a conflict resolution scheme should be seen as a prominent future work direction for UCAT. Similarly, a further effort is required to represent hierarchical structures and mutually exclusive roles. In both cases it is required to account for relationships between roles. Thereby, special role entities should be introduced, so it becomes possible to form policies of a type $@_{req}\langle has\text{-}role \rangle role\_name$.

Our framework can also represent many relationship-based models. Obviously, it can mimic classic ReBAC systems. Additionally, it can be used to substitute some of ReBAC's extensions. CollAC, a model for collaborative access control, introduces additional free variables to account for relations between objects and users. For instance, a Data Host variable is defined for a user, who hosts the data. In UCAT it gets easy to account for such relationships: one can define $\langle data\text{-}host \rangle$dobj relation from a user to an object. Similarly, UCAT can account for between-object relations, as it is done in OOReBAC. For instance, to grant access to a co-author to a new version of a document, one can use the following policy: $@_{dobj}\langle -new\text{-}version \rangle \langle -author \rangle \langle co\text{-}author \rangle$req. An interesting challenge arise: how can one account for multiple nested relationships? For instance, let's consider a situation when we have several versions of one document. We have a policy for the first document $@_{dobj}\langle -author \rangle$req, which grants access to the document to its authors. How can one specify a policy that would grant access to all subsequent versions of the document? One of the workarounds is to introduce an additional relation $\langle has\text{-}root \rangle$ for each descendant. We consider the development of a more general approach to be a prominent future work direction.

Our work goes in line with a spirit of Barker's approach [3]. Barker proposed to elicit a small number of access control primitives and to build a general access control model. Unsurprisingly for us, the proposed primitive was category.

Similarly to our work, Barker notes that the notion of roles in RBAC is merely a type of a category. To achieve his goal the author introduces the rule language based on constraint logic programming. In our work we approached the problem differently. Similarly to Barker we noticed the possibility of a generalized model. We also came up with the notion of categories. However, we were guided by a different motivation. First, we wanted to make it possible for users to specify their local "user-perspective" policies, to allow for local policy evaluation. Thereby, we developed a model based on hybrid logic. Second, we aimed to make an easy-to-use solution. Being guided by the evidence from cognitive science on ubiquity of categorization in human reasoning, we chose category as an appropriate primitive for a usable access control model. Given the evident interconnection between Barker's and our works, it seems interesting to investigate the question of general access control models. In that case, one can specifically consider questions of local and global policies together with administrative models for such systems.

8   Conclusion

In this paper we introduced UCAT, an access control framework based on uniform categorization. Our work is a generalization of the ReBAC family models. In accordance with the evidence from cognitive science on ubiquity of categorization in human reasoning, we state that a user should be able to categorize not only subjects (e.g. friends and colleagues), but also objects. In our work we define such a model, provide use-case scenarios and evaluate it in the context of a scholarly publishing system. Our results suggest that the model can be an appropriate fit for many applications.

We envision that our work can have many beneficial applications. In many real-life scenarios categories can be a suitable access control primitive, replacing roles, groups, relationships. Thereby, as a prominent research direction we foresee the adoption of uniform categories as the basic primitive for the existing models such as RBAC and ReBAC. Additionally, it is interesting to investigate the question of the combination of global and local access control policies and to develop administrative models for the UCAT framework. We believe that these questions might lead to a more general user-centric access control model.

Acknowledgements. This work was co-funded by the European Research Council for the project ScienceGRAPH (Grant agreement ID: 819536) and the TIB Leibniz Information Centre for Science and Technology.

References

1. Ahmed, T., Patwa, F., Sandhu, R.: Object-to-object relationship-based access control: model and multi-cloud demonstration. In: 2016 IEEE 17th International Conference on Information Reuse and Integration (IRI), pp. 297–304. IEEE (2016)
2. Augoustinos, M., Walker, I., Donaghue, N.: Social Cognition: An Integrated Introduction. Sage (2014)

3. Barker, S.: The next 700 access control models or a unifying meta-model? In: Proceedings of the 14th ACM Symposium on Access Control Models and Technologies, SACMAT 2009, pp. 187–196. Association for Computing Machinery, New York, NY, USA (2009). https://doi.org/10.1145/1542207.1542238

4. Bell, D.E., Padula, L.J.L.: Secure computer system: unified exposition and multics interpretation (1976)

5. Blackburn, P., Seligman, J.: Hybrid languages. J. Logic Lang. Inform. **4**, 251–272 (1995)

6. Bruns, G., Fong, P.W., Siahaan, I., Huth, M.: Relationship-based access control: its expression and enforcement through hybrid logic. In: Proceedings of the Second ACM Conference on Data and Application Security and Privacy, pp. 117–124 (2012)

7. Carminati, B., Ferrari, E., Heatherly, R., Kantarcioglu, M., Thuraisingham, B.: A semantic web based framework for social network access control. In: Proceedings of the 14th ACM Symposium on Access Control Models and Technologies, pp. 177–186 (2009)

8. Carminati, B., Ferrari, E., Heatherly, R., Kantarcioglu, M., Thuraisingham, B.: Semantic web-based social network access control. Comput. Secur. **30**(2–3), 108–115 (2011)

9. Crampton, J., Sellwood, J.: Relationships, paths and principal matching: a new approach to access control. arXiv preprint arXiv:1505.07945 (2015)

10. Damen, S., Hartog, J., Zannone, N.: CollAc: collaborative access control, pp. 142–149 (2014). https://doi.org/10.1109/CTS.2014.6867557

11. Denning, D.E.: A lattice model of secure information flow. Commun. ACM **19**(5), 236–243 (1976)

12. Eysenck, M.W., Brysbaert, M.: Fundamentals of Cognition. Routledge (2018)

13. Ferraiolo, D.F., Barkley, J.F., Kuhn, D.R.: A role-based access control model and reference implementation within a corporate intranet. ACM Trans. Inf. Syst. Secur. (TISSEC) **2**(1), 34–64 (1999)

14. Fong, P.W.: Relationship-based access control: protection model and policy language. In: Proceedings of the first ACM Conference on Data and Application Security and Privacy, pp. 191–202 (2011)

15. Hagberg, A.A., Schult, D.A., Swart, P.J.: Exploring network structure, dynamics, and function using NetworkX. In: Varoquaux, G., Vaught, T., Millman, J. (eds.) Proceedings of the 7th Python in Science Conference, Pasadena, CA, USA, pp. 11–15 (2008)

16. Leskovec, J., Kleinberg, J., Faloutsos, C.: Graph evolution: densification and shrinking diameters. ACM Trans. Knowl. Discovery Data (TKDD) **1**(1), 2-es (2007)

17. Paci, F., Squicciarini, A., Zannone, N.: Survey on access control for community-centered collaborative systems. ACM Comput. Surv. (CSUR) **51**(1), 1–38 (2018)

18. Tolone, W., Ahn, G.J., Pai, T., Hong, S.P.: Access control in collaborative systems. ACM Comput. Surv. (CSUR) **37**(1), 29–41 (2005)

19. Wilkinson, M.D., et al.: The fair guiding principles for scientific data management and stewardship. Sci. Data **3**(1), 1–9 (2016)

Collectively Enhancing IoT Security: A Privacy-Aware Crowd-Sourcing Approach

Markus Dahlmanns[1]([✉]) [iD], Roman Matzutt[1,2] [iD], Chris Dax[1] [iD],
and Klaus Wehrle[1] [iD]

[1] Communication and Distributed Systems, RWTH Aachen University,
Aachen, Germany
{dahlmanns,matzutt,dax,wehrle}@comsys.rwth-aachen.de
[2] Data Protection and Sovereignty, Fraunhofer FIT, Aachen, Germany

Abstract. Security configurations remain challenging for trained administrators. Nowadays, due to the advent of the Internet of Things (IoT), untrained users operate numerous and heterogeneous Internet-facing services in manifold use case-specific scenarios. In this work, we close the growing gap between the complexity of IoT security configuration and the expertise of the affected users. To this end, we propose ColPSA, a platform for **col**lective and **p**rivacy-aware **s**ecurity **a**dvice that allows users to optimize their configuration by exchanging information about what security can be realized given their IoT deployment and scenario.

1 Introduction

The success of the Internet of Things (IoT) and its flavors, e.g., Smart Home and the Industrial IoT (IIoT), lead to a surge of Internet-connected devices and services handling sensitive data [14,17,27], which must be secured against unwanted access, eavesdropping, and overtakes. Yet, keeping networked devices secure remains a difficult and error-prone task even for trained system administrators [15]. In the IoT, the situation gets even worse as the intended users have less knowledge about IT security. Moreover, IoT deployments are increasingly complex and consist of numerous and heterogeneous components [17,27]. Simultaneously, these components do not implement all security features [7], e.g., to reduce costs. Finally, IoT deployments are constrained by individual use cases, e.g., requiring or denying remote access. Overall, best practices for secure configurations cannot be transferred easily from one IoT deployment to another. As a result, IoT deployments have often proved to be notoriously insecure in the past [3,4,18,30] or relying on compromised placeholder certificates [4,5].

The goal of this work is to close this critical gap between the knowledge and effort required to securely configure IoT deployments and the end-users' capabilities to *realize* such a secure configuration based on their individual needs. To achieve this goal, we enable end-users to *exchange knowledge about realizable security configurations* in an automated fashion. In this paper, we present

M. Mosbah et al. (Eds.): FPS 2023, LNCS 14552, pp. 15–27, 2024.
https://doi.org/10.1007/978-3-031-57540-2_2

ColPSA, our central platform for **col**lective and **p**rivacy-**a**ware **s**ecurity **a**dvice. ColPSA learns the most secure configuration for any specific IoT component in a particular scenario by regularly crowd-sourcing reports from participating end-users. Based on this knowledge, ColPSA then notifies users with improvable security configurations on how to optimize their IoT deployments.

2   Security Configuration Goals and Pitfalls

Introducing *IoT components*, i.e., a potentially diverse subset of IoT devices and services, in their network requires users to actively maintain end-to-end security and access control. Here, users have to familiarize themselves with a multitude of available protocols. We give an overview of selected IoT protocols, i.e., TLS for secure communication, which can in turn be used by, e.g., MQTT, and OPC UA.

TLS and MQTT: TLS establishes confidential, integrity-protected, and au-breakthenticated connections [25]. Thus, many IoT protocols, e.g., MQTT, nowadays rely on TLS (or derivatives such as DTLS for UDP connections) as well [4]. However, *users are responsible for using up-to-date TLS configurations*, i.e., protocol version, cipher suite, and cryptographic primitives of their certificates [10,29]. Additionally, to prevent unwanted access, *users need to manually configure secure credentials* and *manually enable the MQTT broker to enforce access control*.

OPC UA: OPC UA aims to homogenize IIoT deployments, e.g., by enabling cross-vendor communication [3,8]. Additionally, it is the first IIoT protocol with built-in and attested security [8]. However, its security bases on custom protocol features instead of TLS [20]. Here, *users must actively enable confidentiality and authentication*, i.e., enable the correct security mode, and *select secure crypto-graphic primitives*, i.e., select a secure security policy.

3   Users Need IoT-Specific Security Advice

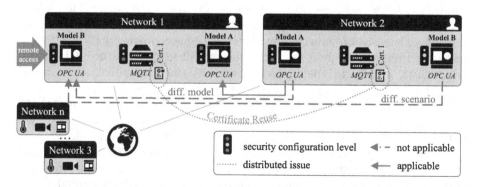

Fig. 1. Users operate their IoT deployments. Security configurations cannot be transferred between devices of different models or used in different scenarios. Additionally, deployments can suffer from distributed issues.

The idea of supporting users with security advice has already been pursued for traditional IT services. However, the shift to the IoT comes with new challenges.

Figure 1 illustrates multiple users operating their IoT deployments that consist of multiple components each. These deployments incorporate both *heterogeneous IoT devices* with varying capabilities that satisfy *different, incompatible scenarios*, and have *varying degrees of realized security configurations*.

Heterogeneous IoT Devices: The heterogeneity of IoT devices highly complicates their (secure) configuration [28] as they typically do not implement all security features and cryptographic primitives defined for a protocol [7,11], e.g., to reduce development costs or due to hardware limitations. Instead, users have to keep the exact models of their IoT devices in mind when aiming for the most *realizable* security configuration.

Different Scenarios: Besides the device models, also the user's intended deployment scenario influences the most secure and *suitable* configuration. For example, deployments with components that are accessible from the outside may require other security measures than deployments that are only reachable from within the network. While externally reachable components handling sensitive data definitely should implement access control, other components are intentionally openly available, e.g., to share data.

Lax Current Level of Security: Previous research found various insecurely configured Internet-reachable IoT deployments, which put the confidentiality of sensitive data and the user's control over their components at risk [3–5,18,30]. Responsible disclosures related to these measurements regularly surprise affected users, which indicates they tend to be unaware of insecure configurations.

3.1   Requirements for IoT-Specific Security Advice

Users need a reliable external source of expert knowledge that can give security advice that is tailored to the users' IoT components and needs. We identify the following six requirements for such recommendation systems.

R1: Technical Applicability: Any security advice given to the user must be realizable within their individual IoT deployment, i.e., take the user's specific IoT components and their capabilities into account. Giving advice solely based on protocol-specific best practices can aggravate to the user's burden when they cannot implement those recommendations or start to ignore inapplicable advice.

R2: Scenario-specific Adequacy: In addition to the technical applicability, the security advice must also fit the user's intended use case, i.e., the advice must be adequate for the given scenario. The scenario fundamentally influences the best-suited security configuration of an IoT deployment, e.g., a public weather camera does not require access control whereas a private surveillance camera should not be accessed by unauthorized parties. Thus, the security advice should not intimidate the user by making overly restrictive constraints and ignoring the user's requirements.

R3: Security: Any given advice should recommend the most secure configuration that is suitable after factoring in the individual device capabilities (R1) and the scenario (R2). As such, the advice must holistically consider the IoT deployment and detect configuration issues across multiple components. Notably, reusing secret values, e.g., copying example private keys from online tutorials or container images, can significantly impede the deployment's overall security [5].

R4: Generalizability: The IoT comprises vast and ever-growing amounts of different protocols and devices. Moreover, there is no clear boundary between different use cases and the applied technologies; for instance, PLCs are predominantly used in the IIoT, but can also occur in the context of smart homes. Thus, any system for assessing an IoT deployment's security configuration and advising for improvements should be generalizable to support established and upcoming IoT protocols as well as different network configurations.

R5: Data Avoidance: Potential configuration flaws in a user's IoT deployment bear high security risks and require manual intervention by the user. Hence, any externally available information on the user's security configuration is potentially valuable for adversaries. Users must be able to trust that any security assessment of their IoT deployments cannot benefit targeted attacks against them. As a result, any system for giving security advice must ensure the unlinkability between users and their configuration flaws.

R6: Scalability: Finally, due to the ever-growing size of the IoT and users' deployments, any advice-giving system must remain scalable. Namely, such systems must be able to handle numerous large and complex IoT deployments.

4 Related Work

Table 1. Overview of related work. Currently, no approach meets all requirements, especially none achieves the desirable combination of applicability and adequacy.

		Appl. (R1)	Adeq. (R2)	Sec. (R3)	Gen. (R4)	D. A. (R5)	Scal. (R6)
Security Guidelines (e.g. [9,10,22])		○	◐	◑	○	●	○
Local Assessment	Active (e.g. [1,2,31,32])	◐	◐	◑	●	●	●
	Passive (e.g. [13,26])	◐	◐	◑	●	●	◑
Remote Assessment (e.g. [23])		◐	○	●	◑	○	●

To increase the level of security, users require advice matching to their components and needs, i.e., fulfills the requirements identified in Sect. 3.1. However, current approaches do not help completely. Table 1 summarizes our results.

Security Guidelines: Current best practices for security configurations on the protocol level are maintained in extensive *security guidelines*, e.g., for TLS [10] or OPC UA [22]. While this dissemination method for security advice can be scenario-agnostic (R2), typically up-to-date (R3), and requires no data to be disclosed (R5), it comes with significant downsides as well. Most notably, the guidelines are centered around single protocols and are not device-agnostic, which severely limits their generalizability (R4) and their applicability (R1). Likewise, users have to react manually to new recommendations, which limits the scalability (R6). Finally, security guidelines can only cover individual building blocks and cannot identify misconfigurations such as certificate reuse (R3).

Security Assessment Tools: When relying on *locally* deployed security assessment, users can choose between *active* and *passive* monitoring of their network. Here, active approaches, e.g., OpenVAS [24], actively scan deployments for issues and passive approaches, e.g., Snort [26], intercept ongoing communication to extract security-related information. Both approaches are signature-based and therefore avoid disclosing data to external parties (R5) but can be updated as the need arises (R4). However, while active tools can scale also to large network sizes [6], passive tools have to inspect every packet, which increases hardware requirements and limits scalability [21] (R6). Moreover, these approaches do not have a global view on security configurations (R3) and current approaches neither consider technical applicability (R1) nor scenario-specific adequacy (R2).

Instead of conducting their security assessments locally, users can instruct *remote* services to perform active scans of their deployments [23]. The service operators can scale up their infrastructure according to the growing needs of the IoT (R6) and combine the results of multiple deployments, i.e., they can detect security issues on a large scale (R3). However, precisely this external data collection poses significant risks regarding the disclosure of users' vulnerabilities (R5). Moreover, remote scans can only cover (directly) Internet-reachable IoT components and do not generalize to arbitrary deployments (R4). Finally, no remote scanning service can holistically consider the applicability (R1) or adequacy (R2) of its security advice for a particular IoT deployment.

5   Collectively Enhancing the IoT Security

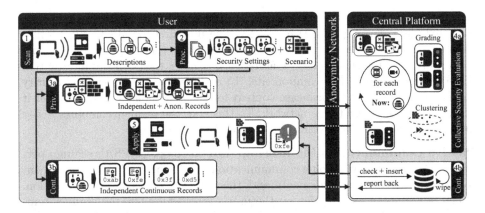

Fig. 2. ColPSA gives security advice for IoT deployments by accumulating knowledge about realizable and scenario-specific configurations from anonymous local scans.

Our discussion in Sect. 4 revealed that current security advice processes do not meet all requirements for improving the situation in today's IoT deployments. Accordingly, we now present ColPSA, our platform for **collective** and **privacy-aware** security advice for the IoT that closes this gap. The core idea of ColPSA is to centrally derive applicable and adequate security advice for IoT deployments from its users' *combined* and *anonymized* local active network scans. This way, ColPSA can incrementally accumulate knowledge about the most secure and realizable security configuration for specific IoT devices and how different scenarios influence this assessment. Additionally, by only processing anonymized reports, ColPSA does not expose any vulnerabilities of their IoT deployments.

Figure 2 gives an overview of how users interact with ColPSA. Each user starts by ① locally scanning their network to generate descriptions of their IoT deployment, including the present IoT components, ports used, and Internet reachability. Next, the scanner ② processes the scan results, i.e., extract their security configuration and scenario indicators, before ③ preparing them for upload to the ColPSA platform. Depending on the data types of individual records, the scanner either ③ₐ fully anonymizes the record or ③ᵦ derives a fingerprint that allows for matching against other IoT deployments, e.g., to detect certificate reuse. The platform then ④ evaluates the submitted reports either by ④ₐ determining the best known security configuration for the affected devices and scenario based on a protocol-specific grading function or by ④ᵦ checking submitted fingerprints against its database of known insecure credentials. The grading function is actively maintained by the platform operator based on the recommendations regarding cryptographic primitives and protocol options from security guidelines, effectively outsourcing the required security expertise to ColPSA's central platform. Finally, after anonymously receiving the resulting advice, the user can ⑤ apply it to their IoT deployment.

5.1   Network Scanning

When joining ColPSA to receive security advice, a new user first has to scan their IoT deployment (Step ① in Fig. 2). The user first installs ColPSA's network scanner, either on one of their devices such as a tablet or as an additional service on their Internet router. The network scanner then collects information on (a) currently active IoT components, (b) each detected component's security configuration, and (c) the use-case context for each component, e.g., whether it is reachable from outside the network. To this end, the scanner combines *active* and *passive* network monitoring as we detail in the following.

Passive Communication Monitoring: As a first step, ColPSA's scanner performs a passive scan of ongoing communication within the user's IoT deployment to learn about active components and the contexts of their communication. When not running as a service on the user's Internet router, the scanner temporarily uses ARP spoofing to reroute all traffic for the required analyses (similarly to [13]). Then, the scanner extracts (a) active devices' internal IP addresses, (b) the number of communication partners for each component, and (c) whether a component is contacted from outside the user's network. ColPSA does not attempt to derive security configurations from the captured packets to keep the load on the scanner low and preserve scalability (R6).

Active Configuration Collection: ColPSA further learns about security configurations by also relying on a more performant active scan phase. While the short passive scan already unveils the majority of active IP addresses in the deployment, some device might only be active occasionally and not yet covered by the scanner. Thus, the scanner also performs an ARP scan, i.e., it requests a MAC address for each IP address considered inactive so far, which actively provokes responses from the remaining devices.

Knowing all relevant IP addresses, the scanner then performs protocol probing and application-layer scans to detect active services on each device. Specifically, the scanner performs full port scans for all identified IP addresses. Depending on the detected protocols, the scanner can gather more details, e.g., perform multiple handshakes to fully reveal a component's TLS configuration.

Finally, ColPSA performs anonymous Internet reachability checks to support the assessment of the user's security configuration based on their intended scenario. Here, the local scanner relies on an external proxy that reflects active scan requests to the device's IP address or the user's public IP address. To protect the confidentiality of the user's setup (R5), the proxy can either be run by the user, a trusted third party, or an exit node of an anonymity network, e.g., Tor. This way, ColPSA's platform operator cannot link any issues to a specific user.

5.2   Data Pre-processing

After collecting the data, the scanner pre-processes it (Step ②) to retain the information relevant for the subsequent security assessment. Namely, the scanner extracts the types and relevant security settings for identified IoT components, and composes a scenario description per component based on this information.

Component Identification: ColPSA's scanner has to identify all components in an IoT deployment to associate security settings with these components. The scanner relies on established methods (e.g., [19]) that use already collected component information on, e.g., open ports, provided data, and mDNS queries.

Security Settings: Next, the scanner groups the configuration of the running services by device to derive a summary of the security settings and pre-process them for later transmission to ColPSA's platform. We distinguish between discrete settings that can only adopt pre-defined *options*, e.g., cipher suites or used cryptographic primitives, and continuously traceable *values*, such as public keys or certificate fingerprints, for enabling the detection of distributed issues.

Scenario Description: In addition to the configuration of each component, the scanner generates a description of the components' deployment scenarios. Here, the scanner relies on general information about the IoT deployment, e.g., device numbers and fluctuations, as well as per-component information, e.g., it's external reachability and the number of total distinct communication partners.

5.3   Privacy-Aware Data Submission

After the pre-processing step, the user *could* already submit their data to enhance the knowledge available to ColPSA's platform. However, doing so may leak sensitive information about their IoT deployment (R5), and so the user first applies privacy measures (Step ③) before and during transmission as follows.

Wiping Identifying Information: Before uploading data to ColPSA's platform, the scanner removes or replaces data from the security settings that are typically irrelevant for the security assessment and decouples the user's components from being linkable to their IoT deployment (Step ③ⓐ). Namely, the scanner wipes all identifiers, such as hostnames and IP addresses, from the security settings. Furthermore, the scanner creates an individual and independently submitted record for each component, which contains the component's security settings and scenario description. Furthermore, as continuous values, e.g., certificate or public key fingerprints, can still identify a single component, ColPSA separately handles all continuous values in different records (Step ③ⓑ).

Privacy-Preserving Data Submission: Since a direct transmission of the protected records would enable the platform to map records to IoT deployments and their owners, the records are sent via an anonymity network, e.g., Tor.

5.4   Collective Security Evaluation

Based on the records received about users' IoT deployments, ColPSA's platform can continuously enhance its knowledge about the most secure realizable configuration and generate advice for users who can improve their security settings (Step ④). To this end, the platform needs to grade the security configuration, identify the component type, determine the scenario it is deployed in, and subsequently generate feedback. Finally, the platform keeps track of continuously traceable values to warn users about reused or otherwise insecure credentials.

Security Grading: When receiving a new record, ColPSA evaluates its security level (Step ④ⓐ) by grading all security options on a scale from *one* (no security, e.g., no TLS enabled) to *ten* (best security level, e.g., using TLS with the most secure, available cipher suite). The grading function is derived and actively maintained by security experts operating ColPSA based on information such as security guidelines (cf. Sect. 4) or CVE data; this way, the users do not have to individually keep up with these information sources.

Clustering by Type and Scenario: Before selecting the best configuration possible and sending advice to users, ColPSA ensures to only consider applicable (R1) and adequate settings (R2) for the given component type in the same scenario. Thus, the central platform tries to find a matching cluster amongst records received before. To this end, the platform uses the component type already included in the record (cf. Sect. 5.1) and only considers previously received records matching the same type. Subsequently, the platform clusters the new and remaining records using hierarchical clustering and the scenario information as features. However, ColPSA remains modular and the hierarchical clustering can be replaced by any other machine-learning clustering approach.

Realizable Feedback: After identifying records of similar components used in the same scenario, ColPSA determines the most secure option to create advice for the user. However, the particular protocol-device combination of the user may only allow for certain realizable configuration profiles, e.g., Security Mode and Security Policy for OPC UA (cf. Sect. 2). Thus, ColPSA cannot necessarily recommend the strongest option for each security setting, but has to find the most secure realizable combination. ColPSA compares the average of all grades in the relevant records to find a secure configuration that has been realized before as the basis for the advice sent back to the user.

Tracking Credential Usage: Besides continuously improving the security assessment for users' security configurations, ColPSA further utilizes the central information hub provided by its platform to keep track of the usage of insecure credentials, such as private keys or certificates (Step ④ⓑ). Namely, the platform keeps track of credentials that are reused across components and IoT deployments. To this end, it counts how often a specific credential is reported by all users. Upon request, users can request the counter values for used credentials in their deployments and compare whether they are the only ones who submitted a specific credential. The platform occasionally wipes its database to reduce its footprint and to improve its users' privacy.

5.5 Security Configuration Improvement

Getting security advice for all components in their IoT deployment, the user now can refine their security configuration (Step ⑤) while being sure that the suggested improvements meet their components' capabilities and match their intended scenario. Additionally, the users get warned about distributed issues that might affect their components, e.g., reused certificates.

6 Evaluation

Processes for giving security advice for IoT deployments should be scalable and provide valid advice for improving security. In this section, we show that ColPSA meets the performance needs of the IoT and generates sensible security advice.

Component and Network Scan: We show that ColPSA scales well for larger IoT deployments (R6). To this end, evaluate the performance of a prototype of ColPSA's local scanner. We mainly implement the scanner in Python but rely on already established methods for active and passive scanning, i.e., we use arp-scan [12] for device detection, IoT Inspector [13] for passive, and nmap for active scanning to easily support a large number of protocols. We adapt IoT Inspector to offer a headless local operation mode, i.e., we remove its web interface and all cloud connections. Furthermore, we extend nmap with an OPC UA module on the basis of pyopcua. We simulate IoT deployments of different sizes using Mininet [16]. For each scenario, we add a growing number of devices that each run an OPC UA, HTTP, and HTTPS server, as well as dedicated AMQP and MQTT brokers; all these components are identifiable by nmap. Moreover, each device also uses a protocol not identifiable by our nmap version to evaluate the performance impact of unknown protocols. To make our simulation more realistic, all links have a small latency of 0.2 ms. We deploy ColPSA's local scanner on Raspberry Pi 4 Model B connected to our simulation and measure the time required to scan the network. Specifically, we run each measurement ten times and report on the arithmetic mean and 99% confidence interval (t-distribution).

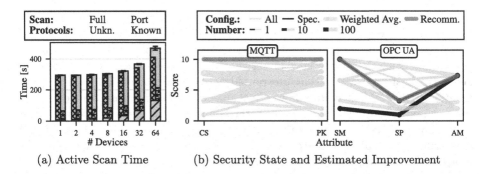

(a) Active Scan Time   (b) Security State and Estimated Improvement

Fig. 3. ColPSA is able to scan subnetworks of different sizes in a manageable time (left) and promises to improve the security configuration of IoT deployments significantly as shown for MQTT and OPC UA (right; Attributes: **C**ipher **S**uite, **P**ublic **K**ey, **S**ecure **M**ode, **S**ecure **P**olicy, **A**uthentication **M**ethod). For OPC UA, it only considers configurations of a specific example device to ensure applicability (R1).

While the performance of arp-scan and IoT Inspector is well-documented [12,13] and feasible in IoT environments, the time required for the port scan and configuration retrieval during ColPSA's active scan is unknown so far. Figure 3a shows that this phase does only take minutes to complete, even in larger IoT deployments, and thus maintains scalability (R6). Specifically, the scan duration only increases linearly from 294 s with only one device, to 468 s with 64 devices. The reason for this is that the protocol identification after the initial port scans is parallelized, i.e., the scanner investigates all components at the same time to retrieve security configurations. Here, ColPSA requires the most time for components using unknown protocols, as nmap's protocol detection probes for every known protocol (more than 2000) when having no success.

Security Improvement: To estimate the potential security improvement of ColPSA, we rely on configurations of real IoT deployments reachable via the Internet based on previous measurements [3,4]. More specifically, we run ColPSA on the configuration of 12 597 TLS-enabled MQTT brokers scanned on 2023-05-27, and 1651 OPC UA devices scanned on 2023-06-11. Figure 3b (left) details the security configurations of found MQTT brokers (gray) on ColPSA's score scale and also the average score over all configurations (yellow). Given that MQTT brokers typically run on IT hardware, ColPSA does not identify any specific type and recommends (purple) the overall strongest configuration ever seen. It recommends users to configure a significantly stronger cipher suite (some brokers use `TLS_RSA_WITH_RC4_128_SHA` despite RC4's insecurity) and a stronger public key to prevent attackers from performing Person-in-the-Middle attacks.

Figure 3b (right) shows the evaluation results for OPC UA. Given that these servers do not run on commodity hardware, not all theoretically possible configurations are feasible on all devices. Hence, ColPSA considers information on the device model (black) and only takes configurations into account that are known to be realizable in this context. For the example device model, the majority of users did not enforce secure communication. Only a single deployment disabled insecure communications and thereby unveiled a better score than comparable other deployments. Hence, ColPSA can recommend disabling insecure communications to all users in compatible contexts. Based on the configuration seen at a few deployments, ColPSA can help to increase the level of security at scale.

Since users are not identifiable in ColPSA, an adversary could *poison* the platform's gathered knowledge by sending too strong and inapplicable configurations. This attack would lead the platform to make false recommendations to other users. As a mitigation, ColPSA can incrementally roll out security advice and collect feedback about the advice's adoption.

7   Conclusion

The increasing gap between Internet of Things (IoT) deployments such as smart homes and the operating users' security expertise requires strong measures to support the users in configuring their components securely. Current approaches supporting security administration either do not scale to the effort required to maintain IoT deployments of increasingly growing sizes, do not generalize to the complexity of available protocols and devices, or only give theoretical advice without taking the capabilities of individual IoT devices into account. Hence, operating their IoT deployments securely remains a big challenge for end-users.

Our work, ColPSA, remedies this situation by automatically learning the best realizable and adequate security configurations by crowd-sourcing real configurations of IoT deployments. Based on this accumulated knowledge, ColPSA is capable of giving meaningful security advice to its users. Our evaluation of ColPSA shows that collectively gathering security information can help to improve the overall security across IoT deployments without requiring unrealistic security expertise from the users and without invading their privacy.

Acknowledgements. Funded by the German Federal Ministry for Economic Affairs and Climate Action (BMWK) — Research Project VeN²uS — 03EI6053K.Funded by the Deutsche Forschungsgemeinschaft (DFG, German Research Foundation) under Germany's Excellence Strategy — EXC-2023 Internet of Production — 390621612.

References

1. Amazon Web Services: AWS IoT Device Defender (2023). https://aws.amazon.com/iot-device-defender/. Accessed 09 Jan 2023
2. Avast: Avast Network Inspector (2022). https://support.avast.com/en-ww/article/use-network-inspector. Accessed 09 Jan 2023
3. Dahlmanns, M., et al.: Easing the conscience with OPC UA: an internet-wide study on insecure deployments. In: ACM IMC (2020)
4. Dahlmanns, M., et al.: Missed opportunities: measuring the untapped TLS support in the industrial internet of things. In: ACM ASIACCS (2022)
5. Dahlmanns, M., et al.: Secrets revealed in container images: an internet-wide study on occurrence and impact. In: ACM ASIACCS (2023)
6. Durumeric, Z., et al.: ZMap: fast internet-wide scanning and its security applications. In: USENIX SEC (2013)
7. Erba, A., et al.: Security analysis of vendor implementations of the OPC UA protocol for industrial control systems. In: ACM CPSIoTSec (2022)
8. Federal Office for Information Security: OPC UA Security Analysis (2017)
9. Federal Office for Information Security: Cryptographic Mechanisms: Recommendations and Key Lengths Part 4 - Use of Secure Shell (SSH). BSI TR-02102-4 (2021)
10. Federal Office for Information Security: Cryptographic Mechanisms: Recommendations and Key Lengths: Use of Transport Layer Security (TLS). BSI TR-02102-2 (2021)
11. Heer, T., et al.: Security challenges in the IP-based internet of things. Wirel. Pers. Commun. **61**(3), 527–542 (2011)
12. Hills, R.: arp-scan(1) - Linux man page (2016)
13. Huang, D.Y., et al.: IoT inspector: crowdsourcing labeled network traffic from smart home devices at scale. ACM IMWUT **4**(2), 1–21 (2020)
14. Khan, M.A., Salah, K.: IoT security: review, blockchain solutions, and open challenges. Future Gener. Comput. Syst. **82**, 395–411 (2018)
15. Krombholz, K., et al.: "I Have No Idea What i'm Doing": on the usability of deploying HTTPS. In: USENIX SEC. SEC'17, USA (2017)
16. Lantz, B., et al.: A network in a laptop: rapid prototyping for software-defined networks. In: ACM Hotnets. Hotnets-IX, New York (2010)
17. Madakam, S., et al.: Internet of things (IoT): a literature review. J. Comput. Commun. **3**(5), 164–173 (2015)
18. Maggi, F., et al.: The Fragility of Industrial IoT's Data Backbone: Security and Privacy Issues in MQTT and CoAP Protocols. Tech. rep., Trend Micro Inc. (2018)
19. Meidan, Y., et al.: ProfilIoT: a machine learning approach for IoT device identification based on network traffic analysis. In: ACM SAC. SAC '17, New York (2017)
20. OPC Foundation: OPC Unified Architecture – Part 2: Security Model. OPC 10000-2: OPC Unified Architecture (2018)

21. Papadogiannakis, A., et al.: Improving the performance of passive network monitoring applications with memory locality enhancements. Comput. Commun. **35**(1), 129–140 (2012)
22. Pohlmann, U., Sikora, A.: Practical security recommendations for building OPC UA applications. Ind. Ethernet Book **106** (2018)
23. Qualys: SSL Server Test (2023). https://www.ssllabs.com/ssltest/. Accessed 09 Jan 2023
24. Rahalkar, S.: OpenVAS. Apress, Berkeley, CA (2019)
25. Rescorla, E., Dierks, T.: The transport layer security (TLS) protocol version 1.2. RFC 5246 (2008)
26. Roesch, M.: Snort: lightweight intrusion detection for networks. In: USENIX LISA (1999)
27. Serror, M., et al.: Challenges and opportunities in securing the industrial internet of things. IEEE Trans. Ind. Informat. **17**(5), 2985–2996 (2021)
28. Sha, K., et al.: On security challenges and open issues in internet of things. Future Gener. Comput. Syst. **83**, 326–337 (2018)
29. Sheffer, Y., et al.: Recommendations for secure use of transport layer security (TLS) and datagram transport layer security (DTLS). IETF RFC 7525 (2015)
30. Srinivasa, S., et al.: Open for hire: attack trends and misconfiguration pitfalls of IoT devices. In: ACM IMC (2021)
31. Testa, J.: ssh-audit (2023). https://github.com/jtesta/ssh-audit. Accessed 09 Jan 2023
32. Wetter, D.: testssl.sh (2022). https://testssl.sh/. Accessed 09 Jan 2023

Comparative Analysis of Reduction Methods on Provenance Graphs for APT Attack Detection

Jan Eske Gesell[✉][iD], Robin Buchta[iD], Kilian Dangendorf[iD], Pascal Franzke[iD], Felix Heine[iD], and Carsten Kleiner[iD]

Hochschule Hannover - University of Applied Sciences and Arts, Hanover, Germany
{jan-eske.gesell,robin.buchta,kilian.dangendorf,pascal.franzke,felix.heine,
carsten.kleiner}@hs-hannover.de

Abstract. Data reduction is a critical aspect of current research in advanced persistent threat attack detection. The challenge is handling the huge amount of data generated by system logging, which exposes dependencies among system entities, often depicted as provenance graphs. Data reduction methods aim to reduce the data size of provenance graphs, but their evaluation on non-public datasets limits the results' transferability and general applicability. This study compares state-of-the-art reduction methods for APT Attack Detection on publicly available provenance graph datasets, exploring their dependencies on graph characteristics and attack detection methods. One outcome of the work is that the effectiveness of many reduction methods depends highly on the underlying data. And secondly, using a reduction method does not necessarily negatively affect detection quality.

Keywords: Data Reduction · APT Attack Detection · IT Security · Provenance Graph

1 Introduction

Advanced persistent threat (APT) attacks are difficult to detect due to their high complexity and long-running, low-key mode of operation. These specialized attacks are optimized to infiltrate a target system undetected, gain persistent access, and prepare for maximum impact [1]. The field of APT attack detection can be divided into data logging, data reduction, and attack detection [4,11]. Data logging of complete system behavior creates a gigantic amount of data, resulting in several GB of data per host daily [6,7]. Reduction methods reduce the amount of data by deleting mainly forensically irrelevant data. The reduced data is then used for attack detection. Many developed reduction methods only consider the reduction rate [3,5,8,10]. However, most important for APT detection is the detection quality, measured e.g. by recall and precision, while the reduction rate and the runtime of reduction algorithms are secondary goals. It is problematic to consider only the reduction rate rather than the impact of data reduction on attack detection, since data reduction is dependent on attack detection and vice versa. Therefore, our research questions are:

M. Mosbah et al. (Eds.): FPS 2023, LNCS 14552, pp. 28–39, 2024.
https://doi.org/10.1007/978-3-031-57540-2_3

RQ 1: What are the achievable reduction rates by applying reduction methods to publicly available provenance graph datasets?

RQ 2: To what extent do reduction methods depend on the data composition?

RQ 3: How much does the data reduction affect attack detection performance?

Section 2 covers related work and Sect. 3 defines preliminaries. Section 4 details the methodology, while Sect. 5 evaluates datasets, reduction rates, their interdependence with datasets, and the impact of data reduction on attack detection.

2   Related Work

In [11], a taxonomy for the field of Provenance-based Intrusion Detection Systems (PIDS) is given. The authors divide the field into three domains: data collection, graph summarization, and intrusion detection. For each domain, a classification of the approaches and systems is proposed. Unfortunately, the authors have not reimplemented the classified reduction methods, and no practical evaluation was carried out. They only present a theoretical comparison.

In [4], reduction methods are compared and evaluated. The comparison takes place on publicly available datasets. Also, the authors investigate to what extent data reduction affects attack detection utilizing various APT detection systems. Unfortunately, the authors do not provide statistical insights into the used datasets. Therefore, the reduction rates and detection results can hardly be interpreted, compared and generalized.

Further, the authors examine whether combining reduction methods and lossless data compression are useful. For the former, the authors noticed that the methods reduce similar data, limiting synergetic effects. For the second, decompressing the data requires additional effort and does not reduce the pure amount of data, thus offering limited problem-solving benefits.

The reduction methods used in this paper are the intersection of the methods from [11] and [4] and are namely: LogGC [5], Causality-Preserved Reduction (CPR) [10], Dependence-Preserving Reduction (DPR) [3], LogApprox [7] and NodeMerge [8].

3   Preliminaries

3.1   Reduction Methods

The reduction approach of LogGC [5] is to erase unreachable data in a provenance graph. For this purpose, the authors defined destruction events (process terminations and file deletions), which can produce unreachable data. Therefore, LogGC checks the reachabilities of the nodes at the occurrence of destruction events, starting from running processes and live files. All unreachable nodes are deleted, as well as their corresponding edges. To ensure that no critical system events, like destruction events itself, are deleted, LogGC further checks that the files are temporary. In the example graph from Fig. 1, the kill event indicates a

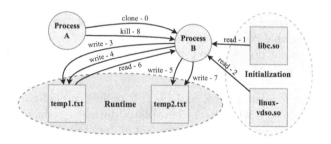

Fig. 1. Example of a provenance graph.

destruction event. At this point, LogGC works through the previous events. In the example, a large part of the graph could be deleted because it is connected to the terminated process. However, this is unrealistic because at least the library files would have other dependent processes and are, therefore, not temporary files. If that is the case, the library files would be retained. Otherwise, they would be deleted.

Causality-Preserved Reduction (CPR) [10] focuses on reducing redundant data using information flow. Each node can be regarded as a status comprising content, rights, etc. Provided that the status of the start or target node does not change, successive events will have the same information flow and can be aggregated. The CPR method is type-dependent. Redundant information flows can only exist within an event type, such as a read event. The functionality of the CPR method can be explained with the events from timestamps 3 to 7 in Fig. 1. The write events at timestamps 3 and 4 can be reduced, whereas those from timestamps 5 and 7 cannot. For the latter, the two events are the same type but do not share the same information flow. This is because the read event at timestamp 6 alters the process's status.

Dependence-Preserving Reduction (DPR) [3] methods include the Full Dependence (FD) and Source Dependence (SD) methods. Both methods also utilize information flow to reduce the data amount, similar to CPR, but considering the global dependencies. The authors transform the provenance graph into a *standard graph*, where nodes store the different states (like CPR), describing global information flows. Data reduction occurs by applying optimizations that prevent the creation of new dependencies. Also, DPR works event type independent, which increases the reduction possibility enormously. The same subgraph for CPR can be used to explain the DPR methods. SD keeps only the first new dependencies to a source node. Source nodes in the example are process A and the two library files. Therefore, the write events at timestamp 4 and 7 and the read event at timestamp 6 get deleted. The reduction of FD would be similar to the CPR method, but with the big difference that the event types were discarded.

LogApprox [7] searches for patterns in file names. First, the file behavior is examined in a training phase for each process. The Levenshtein edit distance looks for similarities within the file names which, e.g., could indicate system routines. The file names are grouped based on their edit distances. A regular expression (RegEx) is learned for each group, representing this file group in the sequel. In the test phase, files that match a RegEx are replaced by a new node representing the file group. Through node and edge aggregation, the data is reduced. In the example graph from Fig. 1, the two files in the purple oval have a predominantly similar file name. Here, a RegEx is learned, e.g. *temp*.txt*. A new file node is added to the graph with the RegEx as the file name. The two old nodes are deleted after the edges have been transferred to the new node. Edges may be dropped during transfer in case they are redundant.

NodeMerge [8] also consists of a training and a test phase. The idea is that processes share similarities in the initialization that a template can describe. These templates are learned in the training phase. In the test phase, after the initialization of a process, its behavior is checked against the learned patterns. To create the templates, NodeMerge first creates a frequent pattern tree. Meaningful patterns are created by deleting rare tree paths and grouping files with similar frequency along a single path. In the example graph from Fig. 1, the two library files occur in the initialization phase of the process. Suppose the two files *lib.so* and *linux-vdso.so* occur together in many process initializations, and a pattern was learned. Then LogApprox creates a new file node and transfers the edges, combining two nodes in one.

3.2 Datasets

A major problem for the comparability of reduction and detection methods is the need for benchmark IDS datasets containing APT attacks. [11] has addressed this issue. The authors' work has shown that most reduction and detection methods have been evaluated on self-generated datasets. They also compared public benchmark IDS datasets and concluded that only a few are suitable for use. The biggest problems are the lack of a qualitative normal behavior, mostly synthetically generated, and thus the lack of reference to the real world. More documentation is often needed describing the recording process, dataset properties, and the performed attack. According to the authors, only three PIDS benchmark datasets exist, namely DARPA OpTC and the DARPA TC datasets from the third and fifth engagements, abbreviated as E3 and E5. The main purpose of the OpTC dataset was to test the scalability of the systems from the TC program. Therefore, the DARPA OpTC dataset is not used further in this work as it can be considered unrealistic.

The term dataset can be misleading regarding the TC datasets, as an engagement is often referred to as a dataset itself but also contains datasets through the records of the developed logging systems. Therefore, we refer to the collection of datasets of a particular engagement, e.g., the third engagement, as **E3 datasets**. We further refer to a particular subset of a logging system as a **track** since, during the engagements, some of the logging systems crashed or failed to work correctly and had to be restarted. Since, reduction methods have rarely been applied to the E5 datasets, only little data exists for comparison with the E5. Therefore, we use the E3 dataset to evaluate the reduction methods.

4   Methodology

In this paper, we only use the DARPA Engagement 3 (E3) datasets. Specifically, the data recorded by the logging systems CADETS, THEIA, and TRACE. The datasets of these three logging systems are the most commonly used in other scientific works [4,7,9].

We implemented the six reduction methods described in Sect. 2 in Java. Due to ambiguities in the original papers, such as non described hyperparameters, slight deviations may occur. The streaming is simulated by querying the events in batches with the size of one million events. Each reduction method processes the incoming events, e. g. storing neighboring nodes. By applying the reduction methods to the E3 datasets, the reduction rates, and the reduced event lists are obtained. The attack detection takes the reduced event list as input and outputs the detection result. For the APT attack detection, we use THREATRACE [9], which utilizes the GNN approach to distinguish between normal and malicious nodes via neighborhoods. Thus, the detection results on the reduced dataset can be compared to the results without reduction.

5   Evaluation

Based on the research questions from Sect. 1, we first evaluate the datasets themselves. Then, we evaluate the reduction rates after applying the different reduction algorithms (**RQ 1**). We subsequently correlate the reduction rates with the analysed data sets in order to evaluate the dependency extent (**RQ 2**). Finally, we investigate the impact of reduction on APT attack detection performance (**RQ 3**).

5.1   Evaluation of E3 Datasets

During the engagement, all three considered logging systems experienced issues during the data collection, like system crashes or logging problems. Thus, multiple tracks exist for all the logging systems. See Table 1 for details.

In the case of CADETS, the logging system crashed and had to be restarted twice while the APT attacks were carried out. The crash times match the ground truth report [2]. THEIA did not crash, but did not keep up with logging [2]. The second and third recordings of THEIA indicate a false set up due to the short runtimes. There are also significant differences between the third track and the others, which will be discussed in Sect. 5.3. TRACE ran largely without problems. Only at the end of the engagement there was a restart. The reason is unknown. Due to its huge size TRACE track 1 required extremely long execution times. Since it is structurally similar to track 2, it is omitted in the sequel.

Furthermore, derived from Table 1, the logging systems work quite differently. The second track of TRACE contains 21 million events recorded within 5 h. This corresponds to the event count from the second track of CADETS, recorded within 5 days. The logging rate of THEIA lies between CADETS and TRACE. The

Table 1. Overview of DARPA tracks from E3.

Logging Systems	Track	Logtime	Nodes	Edges	Avg. Degree
CADETS	1	3d 18h	960,669	12,915,596	26.89
	2	5d 1h	1,389,766	20,606,917	29.66
	3	2d	583,056	7,828,382	26.84
THEIA	1	2d 1h	2,708,401	43,553,119	32.16
	2	1h	117,780	1,470,908	24.98
	3	9h	174,226	915,579	10.51
	4	3d 4h	4,161,732	58,694,406	28.21
TRACE	1	10d 16h	218,7 M. (est.)	750,584,159	6.86
	2	5h	7,611,040	21,914,215	5.78

est. = estimated; Avg. Degree = (2 × Edges) ÷ Nodes

reason why TRACE collects immensely more data is due to the finer granularity of the recordings. TRACE divides processes into process units. While CADETS and THEIA perform system-level logging, TRACE conducts unit-level logging. The concepts of unit-level and system-level logging are described in [5]. Also noticeable is that the average degree is significantly lower than in CADETS and THEIA, except for the erroneous third track of THEIA. One reason for this may be the unit-level logging. With a lower average degree, the reduction possibilities of some reduction methods drop. We will examine the actual reductions before discussing the influence in more detail.

5.2 Evaluation of the Reduction Rates

The reduction rates of the methods on the different tracks are shown in Table 2. Among these, the DPR methods achieve the highest reduction rates overall. CPR can achieve up to 67 % data reduction but is mostly at 30 %. Similar spans are found for NodeMerge and LogApprox, which can reduce up to 30 % of data, as it is the case on CADETS. In contrast, the reduction is vanishingly small on the THEIA and TRACE data. While the reduction methods work well on one E3 dataset, they vary greatly on another. It should be noted that we are only working with the second track of TRACE, as the first track was too large to process.

5.3 Dependency Evaluation of Reduction Rates and Datasets

To explain the achieved reduction rates, we first look at the node distribution of the E3 datasets, Fig. 2. In CADETS, 85 % of the nodes are files, including directories and sockets, 8 % processes, and 5 % netflows. In contrast, the *MemoryObject* is the largest node type in THEIA, accounting for almost 80 %. File objects have a

Table 2. Reduction rates on the E3 datasets.

Logging System	Track	LogGC	CPR	DPR-FD	DPR-SD	Log-Approx	Node-Merge
CADETS	1	5 %	27 %	70 %	97 %	31 %	7 %
	2	7 %	27 %	68 %	96 %	31 %	27 %
	3	6 %	27 %	69 %	97 %	**32 %**	**30 %**
THEIA	1	0 %	**67 %**	88 %	**98 %**	5 %	1 %
	2	0 %	**67 %**	**90 %**	**98 %**	5 %	1 %
	3	0 %	29 %	78 %	92 %	7 %	2 %
	4	0 %	61 %	**90 %**	**98 %**	5 %	1 %
TRACE	2	**19 %**	28 %	78 %	93 %	4 %	1 %

share of about 15 %. The predominant node type in TRACE is the *SrcSinkObject* with a share of 51 %, followed by the *ProcessUnits* with 30 %.

Some reduction techniques focus especially on the data reduction of file events. For example, LogApprox and NodeMerge profit if the dataset consists of particularly many file nodes. The reduction possibilities are thus best in the CADETS dataset and worst for THEIA. However, the actual reduction is dependent on the events that occur. Even if the node share of files is high, this does not necessarily lead to high reduction rates. Most importantly, meaningful patterns or representative RegEx's must be learned, which can be applied frequently.

Therefore, we take a look at the edge distribution. For this purpose, we have classified all event types respectively the recorded system calls from the three E3 datasets into categories Table 3. The file-specific events have been divided into: File I/O, File Descriptor, and File System. Sockets describe the Netflow and inter-process communication. The category *Other* contains mostly logging-specific events defined by the DARPA, having an insufficient description or occur rarely. Figure 3 shows the edge compositions of the E3 datasets used.

CADETS consists of 90 % file-specific events. The remaining 10 % are distributed among the remaining categories. In THEIA the Memory events account for almost 53 %. The reason is a high proportion (over 50 %) of *mprotect* events. The share of file-specific events is less than 25 %. The low proportion of file

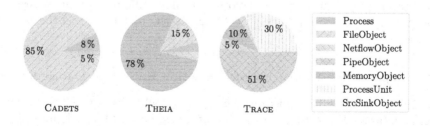

Fig. 2. Node composition of the three logging systems.

Table 3. Classification of the logged events by CADETS, THEIA and TRACE.

Group	Event type
File I/O	read, write, truncate
File Descriptor	fcntl, mmap, lseek, close, open
File System	link, unlink, rename, modify_file_attributes[1], create_object[1]
Process	fork, clone, exit, execute, signal, modify_process[1]
Sockets	connect, sendto, sendmsg, recvfrom, recvmsg, bind, accept, flows_to[2], read_socket_params[2], write_socket_params[2]
Memory	mprotect, shm[2]
Other	other[1], change_principal[1], login, update[2], boot[2], add_object_attribute[2], unit[2], loadlibrary[2]

[1]set of events; [2]events defined by CDM

events leads to worse reduction rates for methods that reduce file events, particularly LogApprox and NodeMerge, as seen in Table 2. While they achieved 30 % data reduction on CADETS, they did not achieve a significant reduction rate on THEIA. In contrast, CPR and DPR benefit from the event imbalance given by the *mprotect* event. Consecutive events of the same type occur more frequently, increasing the reduction possibilities. LogGC is not suitable for the THEIA dataset. Since THEIA barely recorded any destruction events leading to no noticeable reduction. The third track of THEIA must have been a faulty setup. The *mprotect* event accounts for only 9 % of the events and the event imbalance does not exist in the third track. For all reduction methods, the reduction rate here is closer to the reduction rates from CADETS, even if the deviation is not large regarding LogApprox and NodeMerge. The event distribution of TRACE is the most balanced. File-specific events occur at around 45 %, memory events account for 23 %, and socket events comprise 20 %. Even though the file-specific events are almost twice as present in the THEIA dataset, the data reduction of LogApprox and NodeMerge does not work any better. The learned patterns or RegEx's are too specific and do not apply well in the test phase. With adjusting the hyperparameters no higher data reduction could be achieved on CADETS track 1 and on the tracks of THEIA and TRACE. No suitable patterns or RegEx's exist, or the patterns are highly dependent on the hyperparameters, making the learning very sensitive. For TRACE, considering the Avg. Degree from Table 1, there are too few edges per node to group nodes into meaningful patterns. The reduction rate of the CPR and DPR methods is close to the reduction rates of CADETS. LogGC achieves the highest reduction rate on TRACE. The reason for

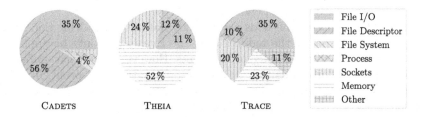

Fig. 3. Edge composition of the three logging systems.

Table 4. THREATRACE detection results.

Red. Method	Red.Rate	TP	FP	TN	FN	Acc.	Prec.	Rec.	F-Sc.
CADETS									
None	0 %	12,851	25,086	324,156	0	0.93	0.34	1	0.51
LogGC	6 %	11,967	26,935	305,238	1	0.92	0.31	1	0.47
CPR	30 %	12,851	26,116	323,124	0	0.93	0.33	1	0.5
DPR-FD	68 %	4	26,411	39,138	17	0.60	0	0.21	0
DPR-SD	**99 %**	0	14,845	6,680	0	0.82	0	0	0
LogApprox	30 %	12,850	23,627	325,599	1	0.93	0.35	1	**0.52**
NodeMerge	31 %	12,850	26,317	322,925	1	0.93	0.33	1	0.5
THEIA									
None	0 %	25,315	68,031	250,754	4	0.8	0.29	1	0.44
LogGC	2 %	25,319	49,742	266,311	0	0.85	0.34	1	0.5
CPR	58 %	25,319	52,485	266,300	0	0.85	0.34	1	**0.51**
DPR-FD	89 %	119	1,263	44,657	587	0.96	0.1	0.17	0.12
DPR-SD	**99 %**	0	3	7	0	0.7	0	0	0
LogApprox	6 %	19,352	50,327	268,456	5,967	0.84	0.27	0.76	0.39
NodeMerge	1 %	25,319	54,854	263,926	0	0.84	0.32	1	0.48
TRACE									
None	0 %	67,383	204,985	939,083	0	0.83	0.252	1	0.40
LogGC	17 %	67,383	231,635	653,458	0	0.76	0.23	1	0.37
CPR	28 %	67,383	275,449	868,612	0	0.77	0.2	1	0.33
DPR-FD	78 %	16	19,959	363,197	0	0.95	0	1	0
DPR-SD	**93 %**	5	34,426	156,884	3	0.82	0	0.67	0
LogApprox	4 %	67,383	257,042	887,016	0	0.79	0.21	1	0.35
NodeMerge	0 %	67,383	202,116	941,945	0	0.83	0.26	1	**0.41**

Red.=Reduction; Acc.=Accuracy; Prec.=Precision; Rec.=Recall; F-Sc.=F-Score

this is the unit-level logging. Due to the more granular system logging, many nodes have fewer dependencies and therefore fewer edges. As a result, nodes belong more frequently to dead ends and can be deleted.

Overall, the reduction methods are strongly dataset-dependent. E.g. reduction methods that specify the reduction of File Events can only be applied to datasets having a high percentage of file events. However, if an event imbalance exists in the dataset methods that utilize the information flow profit, like CPR and DPR. LogGC instead benefits from a high number of nodes with low node dependency, e.g. through more granular data recording.

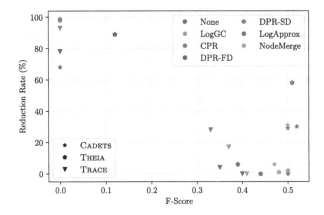

Fig. 4. Comparison between F-Score and reduction rate.

5.4   Analyzing Reduction Methods for APT Attack Detection

To evaluate the impact of data reduction on attack detection, we utilized THREATRACE as an APT attack detection method. The authors of THREATRACE defined time windows that form the training and test datasets for the E3 datasets. The same time windows resp. files were used in this work. The detection results of the three different logging systems using reduction methods can be seen in Table 4. Additionally, the data reduction achieved on the test dataset is listed. The values obtained without employing reduction techniques exhibit disparities when compared to the results from the THREATRACE paper. However, our primary objective in this study is not to achieve an optimal detection rate; rather, it focuses on investigating the impact of reduction techniques on attack detection.

Overall, accuracy is due to the class imbalance of attack and normal behavior, which is present in all three E3 datasets, not a meaningful metric. We therefore use the F-Score for comparison, comprising the metrics of Recall and Precision.

Figure 4 shows the achieved F-Scores in relation to the achieved reduction rates. The baseline for the comparison is the method *None*, where no reduction was performed, neither on the training nor test dataset. Each method is represented in a unique color, whereas the marker type corresponds to the specific E3 dataset used. Ideally, a reduction method reaches a high reduction rate while retaining a high F-Score and is thus located in the upper right corner of Fig. 4. The method that performs closest to ideal is the CPR method on the THEIA dataset. With a reduction rate of 58 %, the method is clearly above the other achieved reduction rates of THEIA. At the same time, it is inserting no loss in the F-Score. Although the F-Scores of LogGC, NodeApprox and NodeMerge drop only slightly compared to the baseline, they are of less significance due to their low reduction rates. A maximum reduction rate of 6 % does not change the dataset size fundamentally, thus rendering the reduction of low efficiency.

The results for CADETS are much more balanced. Three methods, namely CPR, LogApprox, and NodeMerge, achieve almost similar results with a reduction rate of around 30 % and an F-Score of around 0.5. Behind is LogGC, which has a lower reduction rate and F-Score.

The comparison between the reduction rate and the F-Score shows a trade-off for TRACE. With a higher reduction rate, the F-Score decreases. For LogGC, a reduction rate of 17 % leads to an F-Score loss of 4 %; for CPR, a reduction rate of 28 % leads to an F-Score loss of 7 %. Even though the F-Score loss may not seem high, whether a reduction method is justified at such reduction rates remains to be decided for the specific application context. Considering the detection, the data reduction is too high for the DPR methods on all three E3 datasets, resulting in an extremely low F-Score.

The CPR method achieves the best results across all three E3 datasets. The reduction is considerable and often among the highest of all methods. Only on TRACE CPR showed minor detection losses. Thus in total CPR shows a good tradeoff between reduction rate and detection loss. In contrast, LogGC, LogApprox and NodeMerge must be examined application-specific. Even though the methods can achieve significant reduction rates, the successful application is highly dependent on the type of dataset. For example, the reduction rate of LogApprox and NodeMerge is so low on THEIA and TRACE that their use is questionable. Reduction methods that are suitable for different types of datasets are preferable since they have a wider range of applicability.

6   Conclusion

In this paper, state-of-the-art provenance graph reduction methods were evaluated. Consistently, CPR has stood out as the best reduction method, showing a considerable reduction rate while not leading to major detection losses. LogGC, LogApprox, and NodeMerge depend strongly on the type of dataset, especially in terms of reduction. The use of the DPR methods is generally not recommended, as the high reduction rates prevent subsequent attack detection.

A first result was that the reduction rates of the compared methods were very different. However, most methods can achieve considerable reduction rates. Therefore, **RQ 1** can only be answered successfully to a limited extent. The second result is that the reduction methods are highly dependent on the granularity and scope of the dataset **RQ 2**. Thus, the extent of the dependency between the reduction rates and the data sets is considerable. However, this is also due to strongly varying differences in the data recording of the logging systems. CPR is the most robust method, consistently achieving a 30 % reduction rate. LogGC, LogApprox, and NodeMerge can achieve a significant reduction rate, but their application can also be unsuccessful. **RQ 3** can be answered successfully. Despite considerable reduction rates, attack detection is still well possible for the compared reduction methods, except the DPR methods. This is particularly true for the CPR method.

Future work should evaluate the reduction methods on the E5 datasets as the recording systems were improved over the course of the deployments. Furthermore, the use of machine-learning based reduction methods would be interesting in comparison to the methods used in this paper. The use of machine learning methods for data reduction has not yet been applied, and can therefore represent an important next step. It would also be interesting to evaluate the reduction methods using other detection methods.

References

1. Chen, P., Desmet, L., Huygens, C.: A study on advanced persistent threats. In: De Decker, B., Zúquete, A. (eds.) Communications and Multimedia Security, pp. 63–72 (2014). https://doi.org/10.1007/978-3-662-44885-4_5
2. Dynamics, K.: TA5.1 ground truth report engagement **3** (2018). https://drive.google.com/drive/folders/1ATro9_PaoNlg376yA_moI1MbJGF-_HaV
3. Hossain, M.N., Wang, J., Sekar, R., Stoller, S.D.: Dependence-preserving data compaction for scalable forensic analysis. In: 27th USENIX Security Symposium, pp. 1723–1740 (2018). https://seclab.cs.sunysb.edu/seclab/pubs/usenix18.pdf
4. Inam, M., et al.: SoK: history is a vast early warning system: auditing the provenance of system intrusions. In: 2023 IEEE Symposium on Security and Privacy (SP), pp. 2620–2638 (2023). https://doi.ieeecomputersociety.org/10.1109/SP46215.2023.10179405
5. Lee, K.H., Zhang, X., Xu, D.: LogGC: garbage collecting audit log. In: 2013 ACM SIGSAC Conference on Computer & Communications Security, pp. 1005–1016 (2013). https://doi.org/10.1145/2508859.2516731
6. Ma, S., et al.: Kernel-supported cost-effective audit logging for causality tracking. In: 2018 USENIX Annual Technical Conference, pp. 241–253 (2018). https://www.usenix.org/system/files/conference/atc18/atc18-ma-shiqing.pdf
7. Michael, N., Mink, J., Liu, J., Gaur, S., Hassan, W.U., Bates, A.: On the forensic validity of approximated audit logs. In: Annual Computer Security Applications Conference, pp. 189–202 (2020). https://doi.org/10.1145/3427228.3427272
8. Tang, Y., et al.: NodeMerge: template based efficient data reduction for big-data causality analysis. In: 2018 ACM SIGSAC Conference on Computer and Communications Security, pp. 1324–1337 (2018). https://doi.org/10.1145/3243734.3243763
9. Wang, S., et al.: THREATRACE: detecting and tracing host-based threats in node level through provenance graph learning. IEEE Trans. Inf. Forensics Secur. **17**, 3972–3987 (2022). https://doi.org/10.1109/TIFS.2022.3208815
10. Xu, Z., et al.: High fidelity data reduction for big data security dependency analyses. In: 2016 ACM SIGSAC Conference on Computer and Communications Security, pp. 504–516 (2016). https://doi.org/10.1145/2976749.2978378
11. Zipperle, M., Gottwalt, F., Chang, E., Dillon, T.: Provenance-based intrusion detection systems: a survey. ACM Comput. Surv. **55**(7), 1–36 (2022). https://doi.org/10.1145/3539605

Evaluating Deep Learning
for Cross-Domains Fake News Detection

Mohammad Q. Alnabhan$^{(\boxtimes)}$ and Paula Branco

University of Ottawa, 800 King Edward Avenue, Ottawa K1N 6N5, Canada
{malna035,pbranco}@uottawa.ca

Abstract. With the rise of social media users, the quick transmission of news without sufficient verification has become a common problem. The proliferation of fake news across various social media platforms poses enormous harm to society and affects the news industry's credibility. Therefore, it is critical to develop effective automated algorithms to detect deceptive articles. We show that existing models for fake news detection based on deep learning have limitations in terms of generalizability when confronted with a variety of news sources. Current deep learning models frequently fail to generalize adequately across different datasets, resulting in inferior performance. In this paper, we investigate the performance of numerous deep learning models on multiple fake news datasets, each with distinct characteristics. Our goal is to assess these models' performance within the same dataset and across other datasets in the domain of fake news. We aim to acquire useful insights into the models' robustness and generalizability across multiple datasets. We carried out an extensive set of experiments with five deep-learning models and seven datasets. These models are tested within a domain and across domains, i.e., on the same domain where they are trained and on other domains that were not seen during training. Our results show that these models cannot be generalized over various datasets and domains. The results reveal that these models exhibit high accuracy (around 99%) when tested on the dataset they were trained on but they experience a significant drop in performance (around 30%) when evaluated on different datasets.

Keywords: Fake news detection · Deep learning · Cross-domain

1 Introduction

With the growing usage of the internet, the prevalence of fake news has reached unprecedented levels. In the past, before the advent of social media platforms, the dissemination of false information was less common and more challenging due to limited channels of communication, relying mostly on word of mouth or printed media [4]. Fake news refers to the deliberate spread of inaccurate information through social media platforms, often aimed at persuading readers to believe the fabricated content. It is commonly motivated by political gain or financial

M. Mosbah et al. (Eds.): FPS 2023, LNCS 14552, pp. 40–51, 2024.
https://doi.org/10.1007/978-3-031-57540-2_4

profit through advertising [4]. Nowadays, the ease of publishing content on social media without regulation or scrutiny has contributed to the proliferation of fake news [6]. Platforms like Facebook and Twitter have become popular vehicles for spreading misinformation, as they are extensively used by individuals and influencers to share opinions, videos, and various activities [10,12].

The surge in fake news gained significant attention in 2016, particularly during the lead-up to the US presidential election [30]. Consequently, detecting and combating fake news on social media networks has become a subject of great interest among researchers. However, detecting fake news is an extremely complex task that requires sophisticated models to compare and analyze related or unrelated information against known truthful data [34]. The challenges are not restricted to the models used for the detection. The concept of fake news also encompasses various forms, which brings an added difficulty, potentially leading to different approaches and solutions in addressing this issue. Terms like misinformation, rumors, spam, and disinformation are often used interchangeably, encompassing numerical, categorical, textual, and image-based content [5,11,19]. Moreover, the recent developments in natural language processing (NLP) for text generation do not make the detection of fake news easier [11].

The goal of researchers is to curb the spread of misinformation by identifying the diverse methods employed in its dissemination. To achieve this, researchers have turned to deep learning (DL) algorithms to detect and mitigate the spread of fake news [16]. This involves curating or generating datasets comprising both true and false articles and developing models that can predict whether a given article contains genuine or fabricated information.

There are noticeable gaps in the existing studies that were conducted on DL for fake news detection. A core gap is a lack of understanding of the generalizability of DL models that allow them to achieve an acceptable detection accuracy over different fake news datasets. In order to investigate this matter, we conducted an extensive amount of experiments using different DL models across multiple publicly available datasets for fake news detection. We aimed to study the effectiveness of these models in a particular dataset (i.e., training and testing them on the same dataset) and across datasets (i.e., training them on one dataset and testing them on a different one). Our main contributions are: (i) we provide an extensive analysis of the performance of DL models in detecting fake news when they are trained and tested on the same dataset; (ii) we provide an extensive analysis of the performance of DL models when they are trained on one dataset and tested in a different one; (iii) our experiments are the first to compare the performance on a large number of datasets and DL algorithms for this particular problem.

This paper is organized as follows. Section 2, presents the background and literature review. In Sect. 3, we discuss the steps that we follow in our study to build a comprehensive study of the generalizability of fake news detection models. Section 4 analyses the results obtained and answers our research questions. Lastly, Sect. 5 concludes our paper.

2   Background and Literature Review

Fake news is fabricated news in the form of articles, or videos distributed throughout social media which aim to imitate real news media content [3]. Such fake news is deliberately intended to mislead and persuade the readers into believing the content presented [21]. Fake news can be obtained from a variety of tools which include cyborgs, trolls, and social robots [21]. Social robots are what exploit the fake news, and the exchange of discussions among the readers. These bots are initially generated as computer algorithms to contribute to online discussions and continuously spread fake information. As such, fake news is a danger due to its ease of spreading while potentially covering a high diversity of topics and reaching a large volume of sites. This can have a direct impact on readers by touching on topics related to health, democracy, journalism, finance, and social issues among many others [17].

To detect fake news, researchers tend to develop DL models. Recently, more attention has shifted towards the use of DL as opposed to other traditional machine learning (ML) methods. In traditional ML, features are manually constructed, which is a time-consuming task and can lead to biases [26]. However, DL requires a larger dataset to train the model [26]. On the other hand, DL has shown a high detection performance for fake news by automatically extracting useful features. A variety of DL models have been used for fake news detection including CNN [18], RNN [7], Bidirectional Encoder Representations for Transformers (BERT) [31], Attention Mechanism [27], and Graph Neural Networks (GNN) [25].

Researchers claimed that the main challenge in the fake news detection task is the absence of a comprehensive benchmark dataset containing reliable ground truth labels and the limited availability of large-scale datasets [32]. Moreover, only a few datasets are available online for fake news detection, having varying labels, sizes, and application domains [32]. Some datasets consist solely of political statements, others are from social media posts, and there are cases where the source is news articles. This diversity in the fake news domain is a serious challenge. These datasets are collected over a span of a few years and are utilized by DL and ML for different purposes. Some of the well-known publicly available datasets for fake news detection are: LIAR [33], ISOT [2], PHEME [35], FakeNewsNet dataset [32], FakeNewsChallenge dataset [1], FA-KES [29], Fake-or-Real (FoR) [9], Fake News Detection [13], etc.

3   Research Methodology

3.1   Research Questions

To achieve our goals, we propose to answer the following research questions:
RQ1. What is the effectiveness of DL models in detecting fake news when they are trained and tested on the same dataset?
RQ2. How do these models perform when they are trained on one dataset and tested on a different one?

To answer these research questions, we selected five general neural network architectures from the literature and seven datasets for fake news detection. We provide the experimental details in the next sections.

3.2   Selected Datasets

We selected the following seven most popular and publicly available datasets related to fake news:

1. **LIAR** [33]: This dataset is made up of carefully labeled brief assertions, containing 12.8K labeled short phrases. The Politifact site handled the annotation process for this dataset, assuring reliable and accurate labeling. It has six classes: "pants-fire", "false", "barely-true", "half-true", "mostly-true", and "true." We binarized this dataset using the strategy in [28]. The labels "true", "mostly true", and "half-true" were merged under "real" label. We also considered "fake" instead of "pants-fire", "false", and "barely-true".
2. **ISOT** [2]: This dataset's real news cases were collected between 2016 and 2017 by crawling news articles from Reuters.com. The fake news examples were obtained from unreliable websites, which were annotated by the Politifact site. It includes over 44k articles in each CSV file; "True.csv" and "Fake.csv", with articles primarily focusing on political news.
   The dataset contains subjects related to one of six types of information (world-news, politics-news, government-news, middle-east, US news, left-news).
3. **PHEME** [35]: This dataset was collected from Twitter based on 9 newsworthy events classified by journalists. The data is structured in directories. Each event has a directory, with two subfolders for true and fake claims.
   The annotation process was conducted by journalists (human annotators) and each tweet was annotated with one of the following labels: "proven to be false", "confirmed as true" or "unverified". We dropped the unverified data from this dataset.
4. **Fake News** [14]: This dataset contains verified news articles from various news resources. For each article, a label of 0 or 1 is assigned, with 0 corresponding to authentic news articles and 1 to fake ones. There were almost 10k articles in each category. For each news article, this dataset included the article id, title, author's name, text, and the label.
5. **Fake News Detection** [13]: This datasets has about 4k records in a Kaggle repository. It has the news URLs, Headline, Body, and the Label.
6. **FA-KES** [29]: In 2019, a dataset was created specifically to showcase fake news related to the Syrian conflict. This dataset includes a collection of articles labeled as either 0 (fake) or 1 (credible). The credibility assessment of the articles was determined by comparing them to ground truth information sourced from the Syrian Violations Documentation Center (VDC). The authors employed a crowdsourcing platform to extract information from each article, such as the date, location, and number of casualties. Subsequently, the authors cross-referenced these articles with the VDC database to ascertain their authenticity and determine if they were fake or genuine.

7. **Fake-or-Real News (FoR)** [9]: This dataset includes features such as the article title, text content, publication date, and source. It has about 6k instances and it is a balanced dataset.

3.3 Deep Learning Models

We selected five representative DL architectures based on their diversity and recent proposal for news detection where they showed good performance.

Bidirectional Long Short Term Memory (BiLSTM): A hybrid BiLSTM model with GloVe embeddings [24] and self-attention, combined with a dense layer, was proposed in [20]. This model consists of the following layers: Input Layer, Embedding Layer, 4 Dropout Layers, 2 BiLSTM Layers, 3 Batch Normalization Layers, Attention Layer, and 2 Dense Layers. The choice of BiLSTM over LSTM is based on the model's ability to process data in both forward and backward directions, allowing for effective correlation between words in text data [20]. The inclusion of self-attention further enhances the model's capacity to learn the relationships among different words. Additionally, a fully connected dense layer is employed, adding complexity to the model. This was shown to be advantageous, enabling the model to better understand and distinguish between different classes.

Hybrid Convolutional and Recurrent Neural Networks (CNN+RNN): This algorithm combines a Convolutional Neural Network (CNN) and a Recurrent Neural Network (RNN) [22]. Initially, a CNN layer with Conv1D architecture is employed to process the input vectors and extract local features at the text level. The output of the CNN layer, which comprises the feature maps, is then passed as input to an LSTM layer consisting of LSTM cells. This LSTM layer effectively captures the long-term dependencies among the local features obtained from the news articles, enabling accurate classification based on their authenticity.

Convolutional Neural Networks (CNN): A CNN consisting of multiple layers of neurons, forming a complete stack and incorporating an embedding layer is proposed in [18]. Initially, each document is encoded as a collection of one-hot vectors, with the number of vectors set to 500, determined through experiments. This approach ensures a fixed length of 500 vectors. The classification head uses a dense layer with softmax activation. This layer receives a vector representation resulting from the input of a single document as Fig. 1 shows.

Hybrid CNN with Long Short Term Memory (C-LSTM): Kaliyar *et al.* [15] proposed to stack the CNN and LSTM layers in a unified structure named C-LSTM. Because multiple-branch convolution contains varied filters and kernel sizes for successful feature mapping, and the LSTM network provides a batch normalization process, this combination is beneficial. For effectively detecting fake news, the LSTM layer can extract useful information from the convolutional layer. Different filter sizes across each dense layer were also considered. Figure 2 depicts the layered architecture of the proposed C-LSTM deep neural network.

Fig. 1. A CNN-based architecture for fake news detection.

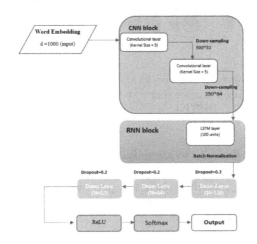

Fig. 2. A C-LSTM architecture for fake news detection.

Bidirectional Encoder Representations from Transformers (BERT):
To address the limitations of earlier fake news detection approaches, which failed
to capture semantic correlations between words, a language-based transformer
model was introduced in [23]. The model incorporates the powerful bidirectional
encoder representations from BERT model [8] used to extract textual features,
allowing for the preservation of semantic relationships between words. We evaluate the usefulness of the BERT in fake news detection context.

3.4 Experimental Settings

Our methodology consisted of two main phases. In the first phase (intra-domain),
each model was trained and tested on a specific dataset. We ensured a systematic
approach by splitting the data into appropriate training and testing sets incorporating necessary preprocessing steps and monitoring the duration of training.
The data split ratio was 7:1:2 for training, validation, and testing sets, respectively. The hyperparameter tuning process involves evaluating and comparing
learning rate, number of epochs, optimizer, and batch size. The second phase
(cross-domain) involved training each model on one dataset and subsequently

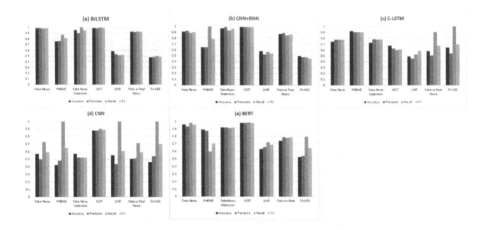

Fig. 3. Accuracy, Precision, Recall, and F1 results for the selected models and datasets when trained and tested on the same source data ((a) BiLSTM, (b) Hybrid CNN+RNN, (c) C-LSTM, (d) CNN, (e) BERT.)

testing it on all other datasets to assess its performance across multiple datasets and diverse domains. The evaluation of the models' performance was conducted using multiple metrics, including accuracy, precision, recall, and F-score. These metrics were selected to provide a comprehensive assessment of the models' effectiveness in detecting fake news.

4   Results and Discussions

4.1   Models' Performance Within the Same Dataset

This section presents the results of training and testing each model in each dataset, i.e., one dataset is used for training a model and testing it. Figure 3 depicts each model's performance when trained and tested in a particular dataset. Our experiments show that the detection models have varying performances, working well on some datasets while performing not so well on other datasets.

BiLSTM achieved a detection accuracy of 98.6% on Fake News dataset, the original dataset that was used to train this model [24]. It also performed well on other datasets such as Fake News Detection and ISOT achieving an accuracy of 95.1% and 98.9%, respectively. However, it was not successful in the other datasets. It achieved a low performance of 47.8% on FA-KES dataset and 58.7% on LIAR dataset.

Our experiments also show that the hybrid CNN+RNN model that was trained on ISOT achieved 99% detection accuracy while achieving a lower accuracy of about 50% in FA-KES and LIAR datasets. The same pattern appeared for the CNN model on different datasets other than the dataset ISOT that was originally used to train this model in [18]. It achieved 88% of detection accuracy on ISOT but its performance fell for all other datasets used.

BERT demonstrated a strong performance in the detection of fake news across multiple datasets, surpassing the other models previously examined. When originally trained on the FakeNewsNet dataset in [23], BERT achieved an accuracy of 92%. In our experiments, when we applied BERT to various datasets such as Fake-or-Real, Fake News, PHEME and ISOT, it consistently exhibited high accuracy rates of 74%, 95.8%, 88.8%, 98.3%, respectively. These results highlight BERT's ability to effectively capture contextual information and semantic relationships between words, enabling accurate detection of fake news instances. However, it is important to acknowledge that BERT's performance can be influenced by the characteristics of the dataset it is trained on. When trained on the LIAR dataset, BERT achieved a detection accuracy of 63.1%, while on the FA-KES dataset, the accuracy was 52.9%. These results emphasize the need for further research to better understand the factors that contribute to BERT's performance variation across different datasets and to enhance its effectiveness on challenging datasets.

4.2   Models' Performance Across Datasets

This section presents the performance of the selected models when trained on a particular dataset and tested on each one of the remaining datasets. Our goal is to observe their performance across multiple datasets and diverse domains. Figure 4 presents the cross-domain testing results (i.e., training on one dataset and testing on the remaining ones (x-axis)).

From the results we obtained, all models achieved superior results when the same dataset was used in both training and testing the model. The BiLSTM, trained on the Fake News dataset, achieved high accuracy (98.7%) when tested on the same dataset. However, its performance decreased with all other datasets, indicating limitations in its generalization ability. In addition, BiLSTM struggled to detect fake news accurately on the ISOT and LIAR datasets which achieved an accuracy of 51.7% and 43.7% respectively, suggesting a potential challenge in handling diverse sources of deceptive information. The accuracy also decreased when the Fake News Detection and FA-KES datasets were used for testing the model.

The CNN+RNN trained on the Fake News dataset showed a competitive accuracy of 90.8% when tested on the same dataset. However, its performance varied across other datasets. Notably, the CNN+RNN model encountered difficulties in accurately identifying fake news in both the LIAR and Fake News Detection datasets. This pattern persisted even when the model was trained on other datasets, such as Fake-or-Real News, where it achieved an accuracy of 87.3% when evaluated on the same dataset. However, when tested on the FA-KES dataset, the accuracy dropped significantly to 25.1%. This pattern also appears in the C-LSTM case.

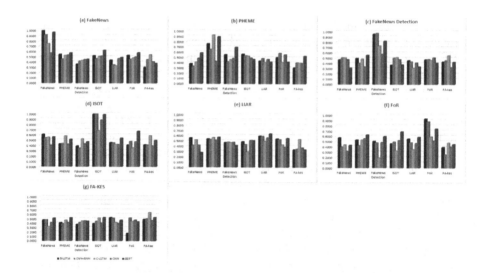

Fig. 4. Accuracy results for the cross-domain testing, (Training on: (a) Fake News, (b) PHEME, (c) Fake News Detection, (d) ISOT, (e) LIAR, (f) FoR, (g) FA-KES)

Notably, BERT's performance varied across datasets, suggesting that dataset characteristics can influence its effectiveness. Despite this variation, BERT consistently outperformed other models, demonstrating its robustness and effectiveness in fake news detection. BERT achieved competitive accuracy rates, including Fake News (95.8%) and ISOT (98.3%) datasets. However, it achieved an accuracy ranging between 38% and 62.2% when Fake News dataset was used for training the model and it was tested on the other datasets. These findings showcase the importance of utilizing advanced language representation models like BERT to enhance the accuracy and reliability of fake news detection systems.

4.3 Research Questions' Answers

From the extensive experiments we run, the defined research questions in Sect. 3.1 can be answered as the following:

RQ1. *What is the effectiveness of DL models in detecting fake news when they are trained and tested on the same dataset?*

The selected detection models exhibit a notable pattern in their performance: they tend to work well on specific datasets but perform poorly on others. This indicates that the effectiveness of these models in detecting fake news is highly dependent on the characteristics of the dataset they are trained on. For example, BiLSTM and hybrid CNN+RNN models achieve high detection accuracies when trained and tested on the same dataset, suggesting their ability to capture patterns specific to that particular dataset. However, their performance significantly declines when different datasets are used, indicating a lack of generalizability. In addition, BERT stands out as a more robust model in terms of its ability to adapt to different datasets, although further research is needed to understand the factors that contribute to its varying performance and improve its efficacy on challenging datasets.

RQ2. How do these models perform when they are trained on one dataset and tested on a different one?

Based on our experiments, we observed that the models' performance tends to decline when tested on datasets different from the ones they were trained on. For example, the BiLSTM and hybrid CNN+RNN models, which achieved high accuracies when trained and tested on the same dataset, experienced a huge performance drop when tested on different datasets. This suggests that these models struggle to generalize their learned patterns and fail to capture the specific characteristics of new datasets. Similarly, the C-LSTM model, despite performing well on the dataset it was trained on, faced challenges when applied to other datasets.

In contrast, BERT demonstrated relatively better and more stable performance when trained on one dataset and tested on other datasets. It consistently achieved high accuracy rates across multiple datasets, indicating its ability to capture contextual information and semantic relationships between words effectively. BERT's strong performance suggests its potential for generalization and adaptability to different sources of fake news.

Overall, our results confirm that specialized techniques such as transfer learning should be applied to enhance the model's performance so that they can be used for fake news detection in a real-world scenario.

5 Conclusion

The impact of fake news on readers is wide-ranging, making it imperative to comprehend this phenomenon and explore approaches that enable its timely identification. DL, with its demonstrated capabilities in NLP tasks, emerges as a promising avenue for detecting fake news. This paper sheds light on the efficacy of DL for intra- and cross-domain fake news detection.

To investigate the models' detection generalizability and robustness, we conducted an extensive set of experiments. We studied the models' performance when they were trained and tested on several datasets from different domains in the context of fake news detection. Moreover, we also studied the performance of these models when were trained in one dataset and were tested on other different datasets. As far as we know, this is the first study that carries out such an extensive set of experiments including a vast number of fake news datasets and DL algorithms. Our findings show that the selected models exhibit strong detection capabilities when trained and tested on the same dataset, highlighting their ability to capture dataset-specific patterns effectively. However, their performance notably deteriorates when applied to different datasets and on different domains, indicating a lack of generalizability. Overall, this study provides valuable insights into the performance of deep learning models for cross-domain fake news detection, highlighting the need for continued research and development to advance the field and address the challenges associated with detecting fake news in various contexts.

In our future work, we will investigate transfer learning techniques for improving the generalizability and robustness of DL models in fake news detection. We will study the most effective strategies to achieve this while exploring new strategies that can be beneficial for the fake news detection context.

References

1. Fake news challenge. https://www.fakenewschallenge.org/. Accessed 11 June 2023
2. Ahmad, I., Yousaf, M., Yousaf, S., Ahmad, M.O.: Fake news detection using machine learning ensemble methods. Complexity **2020**, 1–11 (2020)
3. Alenezi, M.N., Alqenaei, Z.M.: Machine learning in detecting covid-19 misinformation on twitter. Future Internet **13**(10), 244 (2021)
4. Allcott, H., Gentzkow, M.: Social media and fake news in the 2016 election. J. Econ. Perspect. **31**(2), 211–236 (2017)
5. Bharti, S.K., Pradhan, R., Babu, K.S., Jena, S.K.: Sarcasm analysis on twitter data using machine learning approaches. In: Trends in Social Network Analysis: Information Propagation, User Behavior Modeling, Forecasting, and Vulnerability Assessment, pp. 51–76 (2017)
6. Burkhardt, J.M.: Combating Fake News in the Digital Age, vol. 53. American Library Association, Chicago (2017)
7. Deepak, S., Chitturi, B.: Deep neural approach to fake-news identification. Procedia Comput. Sci. **167**, 2236–2243 (2020)
8. Devlin, J., Chang, M.W., Lee, K., Toutanova, K.: Bert: pre-training of deep bidirectional transformers for language understanding. arXiv preprint arXiv:1810.04805 (2018)
9. McIntire, G.: Fake or real news Dataset. https://github.com/joolsa/fake_real_news_dataset. Accessed 27 June 2023
10. Gao, H., Liu, H.: Data analysis on location-based social networks. In: Mobile Social Networking: An Innovative Approach, pp. 165–194 (2014)
11. Helmstetter, S., Paulheim, H.: Weakly supervised learning for fake news detection on twitter. In: 2018 IEEE/ACM International Conference on Advances in Social Networks Analysis and Mining (ASONAM), pp. 274–277. IEEE (2018)
12. Islam, M.R., Kabir, M.A., Ahmed, A., Kamal, A.R.M., Wang, H., Ulhaq, A.: Depression detection from social network data using machine learning techniques. Health Inf. Sci. Syst. **6**, 1–12 (2018)
13. Jruvika: Fake news detection. https://www.kaggle.com/jruvika/fake-news-detection/version/1. Accessed 12 June 2023
14. Kaggle Community Prediction Team: Fake News Dataset. https://www.kaggle.com/competitions/fake-news/data. Accessed 18 June 2023
15. Kaliyar, R.K., Goswami, A., Narang, P.: A hybrid model for effective fake news detection with a novel covid-19 dataset. In: ICAART (2), pp. 1066–1072 (2021)
16. Kaliyar, R.K., Goswami, A., Narang, P., Sinha, S.: Fndnet-a deep convolutional neural network for fake news detection. Cogn. Syst. Res. **61**, 32–44 (2020)
17. Khweiled, R., Jazzar, M., Eleyan, D.: Cybercrimes during covid-19 pandemic. Int. J. Inf. Eng. Electron. Bus. **13**(2), 1–10 (2021)

18. Kozik, R., Kula, S., Choraś, M., Woźniak, M.: Technical solution to counter potential crime: text analysis to detect fake news and disinformation. J. Comput. Sci. **60**, 101576 (2022)
19. Ma, J., et al.: Detecting rumors from microblogs with recurrent neural networks (2016)
20. Mohapatra, A., Thota, N., Prakasam, P.: Fake news detection and classification using hybrid BiLSTM and self-attention model. Multimedia Tools Appl. **81**(13), 18503–18519 (2022)
21. Moravec, P., Kim, A., Dennis, A.: Flagging fake news: System 1 vs. system 2 (2018)
22. Nasir, J.A., Khan, O.S., Varlamis, I.: Fake news detection: a hybrid CNN-RNN based deep learning approach. Int. J. Inf. Manag. Data Insights **1**(1), 100007 (2021)
23. Palani, B., Elango, S., Viswanathan, K.V.: CB-fake: a multimodal deep learning framework for automatic fake news detection using capsule neural network and BERT. Multimedia Tools Appl. **81**(4), 5587–5620 (2022)
24. Pennington, J., Socher, R., Manning, C.D.: Glove: global vectors for word representation. In: EMNLP, pp. 1532–1543 (2014)
25. Pilkevych, I., Fedorchuk, D., Naumchak, O., Romanchuk, M.: Fake news detection in the framework of decision-making system through graph neural network. In: 2021 IEEE 4th International Conference on Advanced Information and Communication Technologies (AICT), pp. 153–157. IEEE (2021)
26. Qawasmeh, E., Tawalbeh, M., Abdullah, M.: Automatic identification of fake news using deep learning. In: 2019 Sixth International Conference on Social Networks Analysis, Management and Security (SNAMS), pp. 383–388. IEEE (2019)
27. Ramya, S., Eswari, R.: Attention-based deep learning models for detection of fake news in social networks. Int. J. Cogn. Inform. Nat. Intell. (IJCINI) **15**(4), 1–25 (2021)
28. Sadeghi, F., Bidgoly, A.J., Amirkhani, H.: Fake news detection on social media using a natural language inference approach. Multimedia Tools Appl. **81**(23), 33801–33821 (2022)
29. Salem, F.K.A., Al Feel, R., Elbassuoni, S., Jaber, M., Farah, M.: FA-KES: a fake news dataset around the Syrian war. In: Proceedings of the International AAAI Conference on Web and Social Media, vol. 13, pp. 573–582 (2019)
30. Sharma, K., Qian, F., Jiang, H., Ruchansky, N., Zhang, M., Liu, Y.: Combating fake news: a survey on identification and mitigation techniques. ACM Trans. Intell. Syst. Technol. (TIST) **10**(3), 1–42 (2019)
31. Sharma, S., Saraswat, M., Dubey, A.K.: Fake news detection using deep learning. In: Villazón-Terrazas, B., Ortiz-Rodríguez, F., Tiwari, S., Goyal, A., Jabbar, M. (eds.) KGSWC 2021. CCIS, vol. 1459, pp. 249–259. Springer, Cham (2021). https://doi.org/10.1007/978-3-030-91305-2_19
32. Shu, K., Mahudeswaran, D., Wang, S., Lee, D., Liu, H.: Fakenewsnet: a data repository with news content, social context, and spatiotemporal information for studying fake news on social media. Big Data **8**(3), 171–188 (2020)
33. Wang, W.Y.: "Liar, liar pants on fire": a new benchmark dataset for fake news detection. arXiv preprint arXiv:1705.00648 (2017)
34. Wu, L., Morstatter, F., Carley, K.M., Liu, H.: Misinformation in social media: definition, manipulation, and detection. ACM SIGKDD Explor. Newsl. **21**(2), 80–90 (2019)
35. Zubiaga, A., Liakata, M., Procter, R.: Learning reporting dynamics during breaking news for rumour detection in social media. arXiv preprint arXiv:1610.07363 (2016)

ACCURIFY: Automated New Testflows Generation for Attack Variants in Threat Hunting

Boubakr Nour[1]([✉])(iD), Makan Pourzandi[1](iD), Rushaan Kamran Qureshi[2], and Mourad Debbabi[2](iD)

[1] Ericsson Security Research, Montréal, Canada
{boubakr.nour,makan.pourzandi}@ericsson.com
[2] Concordia University, Montréal, Canada
{rushaan.kamranqureshi,mourad.debbabi}@concordia.ca

Abstract. In the ever-evolving landscape of cyber security, threat hunting has emerged as a proactive defense line to detect advanced threats. To evade detection, the attackers constantly change their techniques and tactics creating new attack variants. However, the manual creation and execution of testflows to test the attacks and their variants generated by threat hunting systems remain a strenuous task that requires elusive knowledge and is time-consuming. This paper introduces ACCURIFY, a solution that automates the generation of new testflows to test the existence of attack variants using machine reasoning. ACCURIFY leverages case-based machine reasoning to find similar already-encountered cases from a security playbook and then reuses them to generate and adjust new testflows tailored to the attack variant in question. By analyzing historical threat data and incorporating real-time threat intelligence feeds, ACCURIFY can generate new testflows for attack variants with high accuracy and precision, validated using real-world dataset. By automating the testflow generation, ACCURIFY enhances the effectiveness of threat hunting and frees security professionals to focus on strategic aspects of cybersecurity operations.

Keywords: Cybersecurity · Cyber Threat Intelligence · Threat Hunting

1 Introduction

With the exponential growth in the number of interconnected devices and the diversity of platforms and technologies (*e.g.,* virtualization, cloud-native applications, telecommunication), the digital landscape has become a fertile ground for cyber threats. This proliferation not only amplifies the complexity of the

The research reported in this article is supported by Ericsson Research and the Security Research Centre of Concordia University. This support stems from a collaborative partnership with the National Cybersecurity Consortium (NCC) under the Cyber Security Innovation Network (CSIN).

network environment but also expands the attack surface, creating new vulnerabilities and opportunities for malicious actors. The sheer volume of alerts ($\approx$20,000 events per second) [2] presents a significant challenge, as it requires the Security Operations Center (SOC) to automatically and effectively sift through vast amounts of data to identify genuine and advanced threats. Nevertheless, Advanced Persistent Threats (APTs) are very sophisticated and stealthy with different sequences and variants that could circumvent conventional detection mechanisms [6]. An attack kill-chain sequence refers to a set of techniques that composes an attack, while an attack variant refers to a different kill-chain sequence of the primary threat that represents how the threat may evolve over time to use new attack techniques to achieve malicious goals.

Traditional reactive security measures, reliant on known signatures and past attack patterns, are increasingly insufficient in this dynamic and ever-evolving ecosystem [15]. The limitations of these conventional approaches have given rise to the urgent need for threat hunting [22]. Threat hunting is conducted by creating attack hypotheses for potential threats and variants, testing those hypotheses, and then uncovering new attack patterns to enrich the detection.

As described in [22], the process of threat hunting requires rigorous testing of the generated attack variants and hypotheses [1]. Indeed, there is a need to test and validate each attack variant through testflows generated by cybersecurity specialists [24]. A testflow is a sequence of structured tests and procedures used to validate or refute the existence of an attack in the system. However, creating testflows for attack variants presents its own set of challenges for threat hunters. These challenges may include (1) the need for elusive cybersecurity knowledge to create relevant testflow to exactly validate hypotheses. This challenge is barely feasible as (1.1) attackers are evading detection systems by changing their techniques and (1.2) the logs are never complete in terms of threat observability, which leads to unsuccessful tests; and (2) the time and resources required to conduct thorough testing. Therefore, there is a need to generate new testflows for attack variants that use new techniques by replacing the old ones that are no longer relevant to the variant in question. By thoroughly testing each attack variant, the SOC team can gain valuable insights into potential threats and attacks, allowing for targeted security improvements and enhancements.

Motivating Example: APT41 [3] is a state-sponsored espionage group that has been active since mid-2016. It uses different techniques and software (up to 59 techniques, 13 software, and 211 relationships)[1]. The threat actor later exploited a variant of the APT41 by using new techniques to evade detection systems, such as Google Command and Control, Google Sheets, and Google Drive. Google Threat Analysis Group (TAG) disrupted this attack variant in [27].

This dynamism in threat actors' behavior drives the need to design a solution to automate the generation of new testflows for attack variants with a minimum of human intervention. The generated testflows should be dynamic and adaptive to the attack variant in question. Indeed, there is no one-size-fits-all testflow for

---

[1] APT41: https://attack.mitre.org/groups/G0096/.

all threats/attacks. Thus, in this work, we target attacks that do not have a one-to-one testflow matching. It is worth mentioning that, we focus on hypothesis testing and we consider other threat hunting steps, such as hypotheses generation and validation [1], out of the scope of this work.

In this paper, we introduce an innovative solution aimed at automating the generation of new testflows, specifically tailored for threat hunting. While the focus of existing work [9,28] has primarily been on devising test generation algorithms, our contribution is distinctively oriented towards the application of testflow generation in the realm of threat hunting in order to effectively generate new testflows for threat variants. Our work enables the SOC team to respond more quickly and effectively to emerging threats and strengthen the organization's resilience against attack variants. It also represents a forward-thinking approach to cybersecurity, aligning with the evolving demands of the modern threat landscape and adapting the testflow to be able to follow the dynamic behavior of attacks.

Contribution: In this work, we make the following contributions:

- We introduce ACCURIFY, a solution for automated new testflow generation to proactively test attack variants;
- We present a case-based machine reasoning using Mahalanobis distance to retrieve the most similar and suitable cases from a security playbook;
- We introduce a testflow generation algorithm that generates new, effective, and efficient testflow;
- We introduce test adjusting as a refinement loop to adjust testflow based on the proactively collected data and the changes in the attacker techniques;
- We demonstrate the feasibility of ACCURIFY using realistic APT campaigns developed through real-world dataset.

The paper is organized as follows. Section 2 reviews related work, followed by the threat model and assumptions in Sect. 3. Section 4 describes our methodology. Section 5 presents the implementation, we discuss the experimental results in Sect. 6, and we conclude the paper in Sect. 7.

2   Related Work

Threat Hunting: Existing threat hunting solutions heavily rely on expert intervention to scrutinize myriad and tedious log files and user activities, generate hypotheses, and then test those hypotheses. The entire task is cumbersome where thousands of log entries need to be inspected manually on a daily basis [22].

Threat hypotheses and their variants should be generated automatically in real-time based on the current system status and available data, and then be tested and validated using an automated reasoner. Work in [17] combined data from multiple threat intelligence sources with low-level telemetry and then generated attack hypotheses relying on knowledge graph traversal algorithms and link prediction methods. Once attack hypotheses are generated, there is a need to test them. The testing process becomes more challenging when dealing with attack variants that need new testflows. The generation of those tests requires not only knowledge and expertise, which are elusive but is also costly in time and computing. Industrial solutions (*e.g.,* ArcSight ESM [4], Falcon Insight [5]) perform attack testing through prescribed cases or handcrafted queries, yet the process is performed manually by a security expert and is mainly static to the defined case. Contrary to those efforts, we aim at automatically generating new testflow for attack variants that have evaded detection systems by using new techniques and may not be validated using existing testflows.

Testflow Generation: Testflow generation is a critical aspect in different fields (*e.g.,* software development, aerospace, automotive). It empowers the exploration of complex scenarios, including edge cases that might be overlooked in manual testing [20]. The concept tends to generate different testflow, *i.e.* test units, to ensure the reliability and robustness of a system. Various techniques can be used to generate testflows, such as rule-based approaches, template-based approaches, and ML-based approaches [9,28]. In cybersecurity, a testflow refers to a sequence of systematic procedures, followed according to a pre-defined order, to test and evaluate a security posture. In this work, we aim to bring testflow generation to threat hunting. In contrast to work in [24] that proposed the use of prescribed (ready-to-execute) workflows to test hypotheses, we aim at automating the generation of new testflows in order to proactively test attack variants that integrate new techniques in their kill-chain sequence by leveraging previously encountered attack cases from a security playbook.

Security Playbook: A security playbook is a set of step-by-step or ready-to-use template documents that describe exemplary actions related to specific scenarios (*e.g.,* security incidents) [26]. Playbooks are commonly used in Incident Response to ensure the organization can react appropriately and effectively to threats. Based on the Integrated Adaptive Cyber Defense (IACD) Framework [16], different standardization efforts related to cybersecurity playbook have been introduced (*e.g.,* COPS, CACAO, and RE&CT Framework). A playbook may include information related to: (i) strategies for exploring suspicious activities or behaviors, (ii) guidelines for researching new threats, (iii) procedures for conducting threat intelligence analysis, and (iv) steps for identifying potential weaknesses.

Machine Reasoning: Few attempts have been presented to automate the hunting process, draw conclusions, and construct explanations using existing knowledge [7,24,25]. Those solutions use logic-based deductive inference rules following the Horn-clause style and semantic web rule language. Unlike those efforts, we aim to generate new testflows adaptively and responsibly based on the already-encountered cases and according to the attack variant in question.

3 Threat Model

The In-scope Threats: The in-scope threats include variants of existing APTs that are launched by either external attackers or insiders through exploiting misconfigurations or vulnerabilities in the network (*e.g.,* enterprise, virtualized, or telecom networks).

The Out-of-Scope Threats: The out-of-scope threats include any attacks that may be effectively prevented through security patches, firewalls, intrusion prevention systems, etc. We also exclude the completely new APTs from our threat model. It is worth highlighting that the detection itself is out of the scope of this work.

Assumptions: We assume attacks are represented using MITRE ATT&CK techniques [18], thus we do not investigate techniques that have already been observed and captured in the system telemetry. Instead, we investigate techniques that might happen in the attack variant kill-chain sequence. In addition, as not all techniques have been observed, the generated testflow should be adaptive to the attack variant in question. Therefore, we assume there is no one-to-one matching between an attack variant and testflows in the playbook. Finally, due to resources/privileges constraints, we assume that not all tests are executable, which makes the generation of accurate testflow challenging.

4 Automated New Testflow Generation

4.1 High-Level Overview

Figure 1 illustrates a high-level overview of ACCURIFY. SOC admins, after receiving a list of hypotheses (*e.g.,* from a security tool [17] or manually generated [22]), decide to investigate attack variants using alternative testflows. The SOC admins, therefore, send the list of hypotheses to ACCURIFY (Step ①). Each hypothesis is fed to the similarity-based case selection. As attackers use similar techniques from previous/other attacks [27] to change their behavior while maintaining the same objective, a similarity-based approach is used to retrieve the

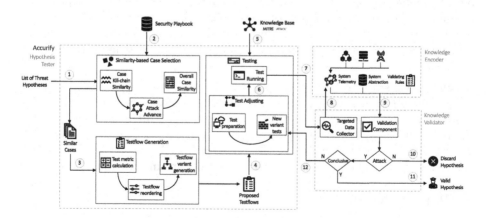

Fig. 1. Overview architecture of ACCURIFY.

most similar cases (Step ②) from the playbook (see Sect. 4.2). The playbook is a database that contains a list of handcrafted tests to be conducted for each known and validated APT with different kill-chains advance. It is worth mentioning that these handcrafted testflows are ineffective in testing new attack variants as the testflows for these variants do not exist in the playbook.

Retrieved cases are then reused (Step ③) to generate new testflows suitable for the attack variant in question [20]. Based on the involved techniques in the attack kill-chain, ACCURIFY selects the most relevant tests (from all retrieved cases) to be executed based on an assessment score (see Sect. 4.3). The new testflow is then fed to the Testing (Step ④). The latter uses a Knowledge Base (KB) – a centralized repository that compiles various information about security threats such as tactics and techniques, (Step ⑤) to adjust the list of tests to be executed according to the system status and the attack advance. The attack advance refers to the progression/development of the attack. The generated testflow is then sent to the Test Running (Step ⑥). The Test Running is assisted by Test Adjusting to refine testflow for the attack variant in question. The Test Adjusting amends the chaining of tests by adding or removing new tests according to the involved attack's techniques. The Test Running then executes each test in the testflow using Targeted Data Collector (Step ⑦) in order to proactively collect additional data and artifacts [24]. The Targeted Data Collector instantiates remote agents (*e.g.,* Endpoint Detection & Response) at different nodes based on the instructions listed in the testflow to collect additional data (Step ⑧). The Validation Component (Step ⑨) either refutes, validates, or refines the hypothesis (Steps ⑩–⑫). It is worth highlighting that the objective of ACCURIFY is to generate new testflow to automate attack variants testing, hence, Targeted Data Collector and Validation Components are out of the scope of this work.

Illustrative Example: The SOC team receives a sophisticated variant of `APTx`. The SOC team uses the defined tests in the playbook, *e.g.,* `Test10` "malware scanning" to test "spearphishing attachment". However, the testing finds no conclusive (*i.e.* confident) evidence of an attack as the attackers use new techniques instead of `T1566.01` "Spearphishing Attachment". Indeed, the attacker substitutes the technique `T1566.01` by other techniques, such as `T1078` "Valid Accounts", and `T1547` "Boot or Logon Autostart Execution". Therefore, as the test for `T1566.01` is no longer valid, ACCURIFY generates new testflows for the new attack variant. The newly generated testflow uses tests for techniques similar to `T1566`, namely `T1078` and `T1547`. The new testflow then replaces `Test10` testing "spearphishing attachment" by `Test36` for "credential dumping and analysis" and `Test67` for "registry analysis". The newly generated testflow then would validate the new attack variant. Later on, if any test fails (*e.g.,* due to environment constraints), ACCURIFY adjusts the testflow accordingly by adding new tests based on the next highest scores and performs a second testing iteration, such as `Test53` for "finding credential abuse" and `Test16` for "boot persistence".

Design Challenges: (1) *Adjusting testflow for threat variants:* as cyber threats evolve, so must the testflows designed for attack variants. Due to the difficulty in coming up with similarity scores for tests that could be substituted, ACCURIFY applies a refinement loop to adjust testflows based on the attacker's techniques; (2) *Automating testflow generation:* as one-size-fits-all testflow is no longer suitable for all attack hypotheses, automatically generating new testflows for attack variants requires adaptation to evolving threat landscapes. ACCURIFY automates the process by employing case-based machine reasoning.

4.2 Similarity-Based Case Selection

To automatically generate new testflows, ACCURIFY starts by finding already-encountered and approved cases by security experts that are similar to the variant in question and then generating new testflows that are more suitable and relevant to the attack variant. A case in a playbook refers to an encapsulated state of an already encountered attack described along with the associated kill-chain sequence and tests in the playbook.

Contrary to Incident Response [26] where playbooks are triggered *reactively* and used to lead the incident response team during a security breach, *i.e.* attack already happened, we use playbooks in threat hunting to guiding security hunters in their *proactive* testing, *i.e.* an attack might be lurking.

Example 1. Table 1 shows an example of a playbook used by ACCURIFY. Each entry represents a case that defines the related APT name, attack kill-chain (*i.e.* list of exercised techniques), and a set of tests along with their order/sequence expressed in Horn clause format. We further extended the case with metrics as detailed in the next sub-section.

Table 1. An illustrative example of Playbook used by ACCURIFY.

APT	Kill-chain	Tests	Metrics {Conclusively Level, Number of Defects Detected, Total Number of Runs, Execution Time}	
APT X	Kill-chain Seq 1	{Test10 → Test16 → Test19}	Test10: {20, 2, 3, 1}, Test16: {30, 1, 4, 2}, Test19: {...}	⌐ Case
	Kill-chain Seq 2	(Test30 & Test35): True, Otherwise: {(Test42 & Test43) OR (Test51 → Test53 → Test52)}	Test30: {10, 5, 8, 5}, Test35: {40, 2, 3, 1}, ...	⊢ Playbook
	Kill-chain Seq 3	(Test62 & Test67) → Test42 → Test44)}	Test62: {10, 4, 4, 7}, Test67: {20, 4, 5, 2}, ...	
APT Y	Kill-chain Seq 1	...	...	

Case Representation: An attack variant is an assumption of an attack/threat that might be lurking in the network/system. It is defined as a 5-tuple $h :< h_{seq}, h_{apt}, h_{sim}, h_{adv}, h_{prob} >$, where h_{seq} refers to the attack variant kill-chain sequence, h_{apt} refers to the potential APT name, h_{sim} refers to the similarity score between h_{seq} and the APT definition in a security KB, h_{adv} refers to the attack advance in relation with the defined attack kill-chain in the KB, and h_{prob} refers to the attack probability.

Given the fact that variants differ, we define different cases in the playbook where each case (c) contains an attack kill-chain sequence (c_{seq}), potential APT name (c_{apt}), list of tests/procedures to test the case (c_{test}), and related metrics per test: (i) conclusively level (how decisive a test is), (ii) number of defects detected, (iii) total number of runs, and (iv) execution time.

Example 2. Figure 2 illustrates an educational purpose example of APT41 case from a security playbook. The case is related to a malicious update for popular software that led to APT41. The case kill-chain sequence (c_{seq}) is composed of ten techniques. The related testflow (c_{test}) is defined using seven tests, where each test has a set of metrics. The case is valid if: (Test2, Test3, Test6) are conclusively and successfully executed; if (Test2) is valid then test (Test3, Test5) need to be executed; otherwise all seven tests should be executed sequentially.

Cases Retrieval: Having a wider threat landscape and multiple attack steps over a long period of time makes it challenging to (i) find an exact match (one-to-one match) in the playbook to test the attack variant and (ii) define a one-size-fits-all testflow. Some methods such as finding all possible tests and executing them might help in testing the attack variants. Yet, this approach is time/resource consuming due to the large search space [28], and might not converge to accurately test the attack variant as mapping techniques with the most similar tests is not an efficient approach [24]. To tackle this issue, security experts use their experience on previously encountered similar problems to create new testflows for the attack variant. Thus, we propose a case-based machine reasoning approach that incorporates the captured experience in the playbook and then uses similarity-based measurement to retrieve the most similar cases that might help in testing the attack variant in question. The closer the similarity measure is to the representation of the attack variant, the more relevant the testflow might be. For instance, if a new type of APT behaves similarly to a known one (*e.g.,* similar traffic/malware patterns, communication with similar C2 servers) [27], a similarity measure would identify the resemblance and retrieve the case based on the previously encountered APT.

APT41 (Malicious Update for a Popular Software)	Test1. Find a mock malicious update	{25, 2, 3, 1}
	Test2. Attempt to run a benign payload (like an EICAR test file)	{50, 4, 5, 1}
T1195: Supply Chain Compromise		
T1195.002: Compromise Software Supply Chain	Test3. Create a new service on a system	{40, 3, 4, 1}
T1204: User Execution	Test4. Use Metasploit to attempt privilege escalation through known vulnerabilities	{15, 1, 3, 3}
T1204.002: Malicious File		
T1197: BITS Jobs	Test5. Disable security tools on a test endpoint and monitor for alerts	{20, 2, 2, 1}
T1068: Exploitation for Privilege Escalation		
T1562: Impair Defenses	Test6. Use Mimikatz or in a controlled environment to extract credentials and observe detection	{60, 5, 5, 2}
T1562.001: Disable or Modify Tools		
T1003: OS Credential Dumping	Test7. Simulate C2 traffic over HTTPS	{30, 2, 3, 1}
T1071: Application Layer Protocol	Conclusive (Test2 & Test3 & Test6), otherwise if (Test2) Then (Test3 & Test5), Otherwise all tests sequentially	

Fig. 2. An educational purpose example of APT41 case related to *"malicious update for a popular software"* and related testflow.

Considering h an attack variant as a new case to be tested, case-based machine reasoning uses a similarity function to quantify the resemblance between the received case and other cases in the playbook. Different similarity functions could be used [23] such as Euclidean distance, Jaccard similarity, Pearson correlation coefficient, etc. However, in this work, we use Cosine similarity [29] to calculate the similarity between two kill-chain sequences and Mahalanobis distance [19] to retrieve the most similar cases. The motivation behind using Cosine similarity is due to the fact that it is not impacted by the magnitude of the vectors (*i.e.* scale-invariance), and Mahalanobis distance because it can identify similarity scores more effectively when data dimensions have correlations (*i.e.* consider the covariance among variables).

In [17], the authors showed how different probability values can be calculated for attack hypotheses. We then consider those probabilities for each attack variant, represented as a vector $h = [h_{seq}, h_{apt}, h_{sim}, h_{adv}, h_{prob}]$, where h_{seq} is the kill-chain sequence, h_{name} is potential APT name, h_{sim} is the kill-chain similarity with KB, h_{adv} is the attack advance, and h_{prob} is the attack probability. The playbook has n cases, each case represented as a vector $c = [c_{name}, c_{seq}, c_{test}]$. In order to retrieve the most similar cases using Mahalanobis, playbook cases should have the same features as the received attack variant (*i.e.* similarity score, attack advance, and attack probability). In the following, we present how those features are calculated.

Example 3. Assuming Accurify receives the following variant kill-chain sequences: $h^1_{seq} = $ [Supply Chain Compromise, Update Software, Component Firm-ware, Pre-OS Boot, Bootkit] and $h^2_{seq} = $ [Supply Chain Compromise, User Execu-tion, Malicious File, Exploitation for Privilege Escalation, OS Credential Dumping]. The selected case from the playbook (as shown in Fig. 2) has the following kill-chain sequence $c_{seq} = $ [Supply Chain Compromise, Compromise Software Supply Chain, User Execution, Malicious File, BITS Jobs, Exploitation for Privilege Escalation, Impair Defenses, Disable or Modify Tools, OS Creden-tial Dumping, Application Layer Protocol].

Case Kill-chain Similarity Score: Due to the fact that the kill-chain sequence changes from one variant to another, the case kill-chain similarity score (c_{sim}) is then responsively calculated based on the received attack variant. The case kill-chain similarity score quantifies how similar the attack variant kill-chain sequence (h_{seq}) is to the case kill-chain sequence (c_{seq}). The score measures the statistical relationship (*i.e.* association, strength, similarity) and provides information about the magnitude of the relationship and its direction (*i.e.* positive or negative). The Cosine similarity [29] measures the similarity between two non-zero vectors (*e.g.*, attack variant kill-chain sequence h_{seq} and case kill-chain sequence c_{seq}) in a multi-dimensional space (representing in a vector format [8]), $c_{sim} = \frac{(h_{seq} \cdot c_{seq})}{(||h_{seq}|| \, ||c_{seq}||)}$, where ($h_{seq} \cdot c_{seq}$) is dot product between kill-chain sequences; and $||h||$ and $||c||$ represent the L2 norm or magnitude of the vector h_{seq} and c_{seq}, respectively. The similarity score value ranges from $+1$ to -1. A value of $+1$ indicates a perfect positive similarity (very similar sequences), 0 indicates no similarity, -1 indicates a perfect negative similarity (very dissimilar sequences), and an in-between value indicates intermediate similarity/dissimilarity.

Example 4. Using the same sequences from Example 3, the Cosine similarity score of (c_{seq}, h^1_{seq}) is 0.14142, which indicates that the two sequences are independent. Similarly, the Cosine similarity score of (c_{seq}, h^2_{seq}) is 0.7071, which indicates that the two sequences are related due to the commonly used techniques.

Case Attack Advance: The testflow for a case in the playbook is well-defined by security specialists based on the APT kill-chain sequence and the attack advance. Due to the fact that attackers might change their techniques, it is important to responsively calculate the attack advance of each case based on the attack variant in question. This helps in determining the most similar/suitable tests to be conducted from the playbook based on the attack advance. Toward this, we were inspired by graph theory (graph commonality) [14] to calculate the case attack advance. The idea consists of using the case kill-chain sequence (c_{seq}) as a reference path and then measuring the advance/progress as the degree of advance between the given attack variant kill-chain sequence (h_{seq}) and the reference path (c_{seq}).

In order to quantify the difference between the two kill-chain sequences, we apply the concept of edit distance [13]. Edit distance (*e.g.,* Levenshtein distance [30]) measures the minimum number of operations needed to transform one sequence into the other, where an operation can be an insertion (adding a technique from the reference path into the hypothesis kill-chain sequence), deletion (removing a technique from the hypothesis kill-chain sequence), or substitution (replacing a technique in the hypothesis kill-chain sequence with a technique from the reference path). ACCURIFY uses Levenshtein distance to calculate the attack advance. Using attack variant and case kill-chain sequences, it maintains a matrix to track any deletion, insertion, or substitution in the attack variant kill-chain sequence, and then returns a normalized value of the attack advance.

Example 5. Using the same attack variants and case kill-chain sequences from Example 4, the attack advance for (c_{seq}, h^1_{seq}) is 0.09, while (c_{seq}, h^2_{seq}) is 0.5. This is due to similarity/dissimilar distributions of used techniques in each kill-chain sequence in relation to the APT41 definition in the playbook[2].

Overall Case Similarity Score: Since case kill-chain similarity score and attack advance metrics correlate with actual attack probability [21], the case attack probability is then obtained using the assessment approach (*i.e.* criticality rating), as defined in graph theory [11], and is calculated by multiplying the case kill-chain similarity score and case attack advance $c_{prob} = w * c_{sim} + (1-w) * c_{adv}$, where w is a weighted average for kill-chain similarity and attack advance value, and is chosen empirically in collaboration with SOC team.

---

[2] APT41: https://attack.mitre.org/groups/G0096/.

Once all values (c_{sim}, c_{adv}, and c_{prob}) are calculated, we calculate the mean M of the distribution (playbook) as shown in Eq. (1):

$$M = \left[\frac{1}{n}\sum_{i=1}^{n} c_{sim}^i, \quad \frac{1}{n}\sum_{i=1}^{n} c_{adv}^i, \quad \frac{1}{n}\sum_{i=1}^{n} c_{prob}^i\right] \tag{1}$$

where c^i is the ith case in the playbook.

The covariance matrix S is a matrix where each element s_{jk} is calculated as shown in Eq. (2).

$$s_{jk} = \frac{1}{n-1}\sum_{i=1}^{n}(c_{ij} - m_j)(c_{ik} - m_k) \tag{2}$$

where m_j is the mean of the jth feature.

Finally, the Mahalanobis distance $\rho(H)$ for the attack avriant h is calculated as shown in Eq. (3).

$$\rho(h) = \sqrt{(h-M)^T \cdot S^{-1} \cdot (h-M)} \tag{3}$$

where T denotes the transpose matrix.

Cases that exceed a pre-defined threshold will be considered similar cases.

4.3   Testflow Generation

Once similar cases are retrieved from the playbook, ACCURIFY uses the associated tests for each retrieved case to generate new, relevant, and a minimum-effort testflow for the variant in question. Established tests from similar cases have been explored and have proven their efficiency in certain scenarios [12]. This means that they can automatically offer a reliable new testflow to begin the testing with while saving a lot of time and effort.

By building upon the foundation of testflows from analogous cases, ACCURIFY can ensure both efficiency and effectiveness in the testing process. Algorithm 1 identifies high-priority tests (highest score) that should be executed first. It assesses the relevance of each test (test score α) by examining the metrics from the previous testflows through a weighted priority system – defined empirically in collaboration with the SOC team. This is achieved by ensuring that a test that has led to more defects in the past will have a lower score (line 6) and penalizing non-conclusive tests by inflating (e.g., doubling) their execution time (line 9) and offering an advantage to those that have detected more defects. The proposed testflow might compromise tests from more than one case. These tests are suitable for the attack variant in question and more effective in defect detection or had strong conclusively in the past. The generated testflows differ from the ones in playbook: (1) reorder the tests to have the most conclusive tests to be performed earlier in the testflow, (2) replace some test Test$_i$ in the current testflow with another test Test$_j$ for the similar tactic/stage with higher score value to generate testflows for attack variants. The intuition is that the attacker, to conduct attack variants, would replace the technique T_i with the most efficient technique T_j for the same tactic than T_i.

Algorithm 1: Pseudocode for testflow generation process.

Input: C: similar cases
Output: proposed_tests: list of proposed tests
1 proposed_tests ← list;
2 **for** $(c \in C)$ **do**
3   **for** $(t \in c_{test})$ **do**
4   effectiveness_ratio ← $\frac{t.\text{defects\_detected}}{t.\text{num\_past\_runs}}$;
5   **if** $(t.is\_conclusive)$ **then**
6 | $\alpha_t \leftarrow \frac{1}{\text{effectiveness\_ratio}} \times t.\text{execution\_time}$;
7   **end**
8   **else**
9 | $\alpha_t \leftarrow (2 \times t.\text{execution\_time}) - (\frac{0.5}{\text{effectiveness\_ratio}})$;
10   **end**
11   Add (t, α_t) to proposed_tests;
12   **end**
13 **end**
14 Sort proposed_tests by α in ascending order;
15 **return** proposed_tests;

4.4   Testing

The Testing component is responsible for handling tests either by adjusting the testflow or executing tests at the targeted nodes. It is composed of two main elements:

- *Test Running*: The Test Running is responsible for the actual execution of tests. It executes tests according to the defined testflow. Since ACCURIFY uses Targeted Data Collectors, the Test Running is responsible for instantiating remote agents at specific nodes as defined by each test.
- *Test Adjusting*: The Test Adjusting is responsible for (1) *test preparation*: preparing and configuring the test environment for each test to be executed. It adjusts the testflow and tests data according to specific requirements (*e.g.*, system configuration, test parameters, dependency checks). (2) *new variant tests*: modifying the testflow by adding new tests based on the validation results. If a test has failed due to environment restrictions or a new technique is used by the attacker due to the stealthy nature of the attack, ACCURIFY substitutes the test with the next highest-score test from the proposed list of tests. It is important to mention that tests are substituted within the same attack stage (*e.g.*, tactics) as defined in the playbook, which keeps the testflow coherent and adaptive for new attack variants.

The collected data by the Targeted Data Collector is then appended to the System Telemetry, which is used along with the System Abstraction and Validating Rules by the Validation Component. The latter could be any automated system or a security expert (in this work, we consider the validation out of scope). The Validation Component refutes, validates, or refines the hypothesis.

The refinement is performed mainly when more testing is needed if (i) a test has not been successfully executed, (ii) more data is needed to be collected to validate the hypothesis, or (iii) the attacker is using different techniques.

5   Implementation

Implementation Environment: We implemented ACCURIFY using Python 3 programming language. We performed our experiments on Intel Xeon E312xx, 6 vCPU @2.69Ghz, with 32GB RAM running Ubuntu 20.04. We used Neo4j 4.4.11 running on top of Docker 23.0.1 to manage system telemetry and knowledge base.

Knowledge Base: We built our KB using MITRE ATT&CK v12 [18] and made it available online[3]. We extracted all the MITRE ATT&CK techniques and generated a graph database hosted on Neo4j graph database management system[4]. We used the open-source JSON file from the MITRE CTI[5] and parsed all nodes (attack-pattern, campaign, intrusion-set, tools, etc.) and their relationships into a graph database. The CTI database contains up to 2060 nodes, 27411 relationships, and 366 APTs conducted using up to 861 unique techniques.

Real Attack Dataset: To demonstrate the feasibility of our solution, we used a real dataset [10]. The dataset covers 86 APTs and 350 campaigns from 2008 to 2020. It includes information about attack vectors, exploited vulnerabilities, and affected software and their versions, formed in 7150 nodes, 79118 relationships, and 170 unique techniques.

6   Experimental Results

In this section, we demonstrate the *feasibility*, *effectiveness*, and *efficiency* of ACCURIFY using real-world dataset [10].

Evaluation Scenario: We focus on APT41, APT29, Lazarus, Windshift, and Dragonfly, as they represent stealthy and complex APT attacks – respectively conducted through 59, 107, 111, 34, and 58 TTPs (tactics, techniques, and procedures), through several systems and have potential variants [27]. We split the dataset [10] into two parts, the first part to generate attack variants and the other part to test them. For the evaluation, assisted by security experts, we built a playbook for the covered APTs in the evaluation scenario. We present the 90th percentile of the results collected for 10 attack variants per each APT.

It is important to highlight that existing threat hunting solutions rely on the security expert to manually create testflows [22]. To the best of the authors' knowledge, there is no algorithm in the literature that automates the process, which we can use as a baseline to compare with. Thus, and to further gauge the performance of ACCURIFY, we implemented a greedy algorithm (*i.e.* prioritize tests with lowest defect rate) and random testflow generation (*i.e.* worst-case scenario) to generate testflow using the same playbook.

---

[3] CTI KB: https://github.com/EricssonResearch/cti-kb.
[4] Neo4j Graph Data Platform: www.neo4j.com.
[5] MITRE ATT&CK CTI: www.github.com/mitre/cti/.

6.1   Feasibility

The feasibility refers to the practicality and viability of ACCURIFY in generating new and relevant testflows for attack variants. In order to demonstrate the feasibility of ACCURIFY, we calculate the number of successful tests, the number of initial tests, and the number of test adjustments.

Number of Successful Tests: Figure 3(a) shows the number of overall successful tests used for the attack variant in question, including the successful ones after refinement. Unlike the greedy algorithm, which tests all possible techniques leading to unnecessary tests, ACCURIFY effectively selects new and most suitable tests for the new techniques employed by the attacker. Additionally, the random algorithm produced all possible tests from the retrieved cases disregarding their relevance. ACCURIFY excels in generating highly efficient new testflows tailored for attack variants.

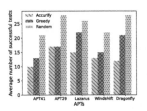
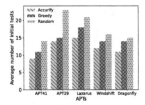
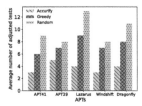

(a) No. of successful tests.   (b) No. of initial tests.   (c) No. of adjusted tests.

Fig. 3. Feasibility results.

Number of Initial Tests: Figure 3(b) shows the number of initial tests selected by each algorithm, excluding the adjusted tests. The results show that the number varies from one APT to another based on the attack advance and set of defined tests in the playbook. Indeed, for all APTs, ACCURIFY was able to select less number of tests compared with the greedy and random algorithm due to its efficient test assessment. The selected tests belong to up to three different cases in order to generate a new testflow. The number of newly generated tests varies based on the nature of the tests (conclusive factor and historical performances).

Number of Adjusted Tests: In this experiment, we considered how many tests need to be changed in order to generate a new valid testflow for the attack variant. We extended the refinement loop to the greedy and random algorithms as well. In Fig. 3(c), we can notice that ACCURIFY requires minimal test refinement compared with the greedy and random algorithms due to its efficient test assessment and refinement loop. The results also conclude that for APTs that have well-defined cases in the playbook or for quite similar to KB's definitions, few adjustments have been conducted (*e.g.,* APT41), otherwise, more adjustments are needed to reach the confidence level and validate the attack variant (*e.g.,* APT29). This is due to the fact that either not all tests could be successfully executed, or the attacker is using different techniques that require the generation of new tests. These results underscore ACCURIFY's efficacy in generating new testflow for attack variants with a limited number of targeted tests.

6.2 Effectiveness

Effectiveness measures whether ACCURIFY achieves its desired outcomes, by successfully retrieving similar cases from the playbook and generating relevant testflow that could validate the attack variant in question. To gauge the effectiveness of ACCURIFY, we measure the accuracy, recall, precision, and F1 score. Figure 4 showcases the effectiveness of ACCURIFY using a small-size playbook.

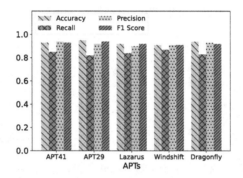

Fig. 4. Effectiveness results.

Accuracy: It refers to the ratio of correctly used cases to generate relevant testflow to the total number of retrieved cases $\left(\frac{TP + TN}{TP + TN + FP + FN}\right)$. The results indicate that ACCURIFY is effective for most APTs ($\approx$90%). The reason for this level of accuracy is related to the quality of the cases in the playbook and its similarity with the received attack variants. The results also indicate a consistent performance across APTs. This is due to the fact that more cases are retrieved (up to three cases) due to the nature of the received attack variant and similarity measures.

Recall: It refers to the ratio of correctly retrieved positive cases to all the actual positives $\left(\frac{TP}{TP+FN}\right)$. The results show that ACCURIFY is able to correctly retrieve valid cases for all the received attack variants. This indicates that the choice of similarity function, $i.e.$ Mahalanobis distance, helps in retrieving not only similar cases but also relevant cases that help in generating new testflow for the attack variant in question.

Precision: It refers to the ratio of correctly used positive cases to the total retrieved positive cases $\left(\frac{TP}{TP+FP}\right)$. The results indicate that all the retrieved cases are used to generate a new testflow for the attack variants. Although the accuracy was not 100% (as attackers use new techniques and not all tests are successfully executed), the attack variants were successfully tested by combining tests from all the retrieved cases (see Fig. 3(a)).

F1 Score: It is the mean of precision and recall $\left(2 \times \frac{\text{Precision} \times \text{Recall}}{\text{Precision} + \text{Recall}}\right)$. The results show that ACCURIFY reaches an excellent F1 score. Yet, still able to test those attack variants after a few adjustments (see Fig. 3(c)). This pertains to the fact that the performance of ACCURIFY might be impacted by the playbook. The score is also impacted by the quality of the received attack variant.

6.3   Efficiency

The efficiency of a solution relates to consumed resources (*e.g.*, computation time, CPU) in achieving the outcomes. To gauge the efficiency of ACCURIFY, we measure: (i) time to generate testflow, and (ii) resource utilization.

Table 2 presents the average time to generate a testflow and CPU utilization under a regular running environment. We can notice that the time to generate a testflow for a given attack variant is relatively fast (an average of 0.03 sec). In addition, ACCURIFY uses a relatively low percentage of the CPU (an average of 5%), which indicates the potential scalability of the solution.

Table 2. Efficiency results.

Metric	APT41	APT29	Lazarus	Windshift	Dragonfly
Time to generate testflow (sec)	0.0446	0.0580	0.0335	0.0337	0.0330
CPU utilization (%)	4.86	5.63	8.32	7.20	5.55

6.4   Discussion

ACCURIFY relies on a trusted security playbook, which we assume is trustworthy and reliable. The quality of cases in the playbook has an impact on the overall effectiveness of our approach. As in recent years, the organizations are significantly enhancing their threat intelligence capabilities by sharing playbooks using STIX through CTI in industry and academia, we believe the quality of these cases will improve constantly in the future [4,5] which in return makes our approach more robust and effective in the future. In the future, we plan to measure the accuracy of ACCURIFY with a large-scale playbook.

7   Conclusion and Future Work

In an era where cyber threats are evolving through dynamic usage of different techniques by the attackers, there is a growing need for a solution that generates new testflows to proactively test attacks and their variants with minimal human intervention. In this work, we designed ACCURIFY, a solution that uses machine reasoning to automate the generation of new testflows tailored for attack variants. ACCURIFY employs a case-based machine reasoning using Mahalanobis distance to retrieve the most suitable case from a security playbook; generates new, effective, and efficient testflows; and then adjusts testflows based on the proactive collected data and change in attacker's behavior in order to further test the attack variant in question. The obtained results using realistic APT campaigns through real-world dataset show the feasibility, effectiveness, and efficiency of ACCURIFY. The next phase of our research is to automate the validation component to close the testing and validation loop of attack variants and enrich the playbook with the newly learned testflows.

References

1. A framework for cyber threat hunting. Technical report, Sqrrl Data, Inc. (2018)
2. Technical Requirements for the ArcSight Platform. Micro Focus ArcSight (2021)
3. APT41: A Dual Espionage and Cyber Crime Operation (2022)
4. ArcSight's Latest and Greatest (2022)
5. Falcon Insight: Endpoint Detection and Response (EDR) (2022)
6. Alshamrani, A., et al.: A survey on advanced persistent threats: techniques, solutions, challenges, and research opportunities. IEEE COMST **21**(2), 1851–1877 (2019)
7. Araujo, F., et al.: Evidential Cyber Threat Hunting. SDM (2021)
8. Church, K.W.: Word2Vec. Nat. Lang. Eng. **23**(1), 155–162 (2017)
9. Dehaerne, E., et al.: Code generation using machine learning: a systematic review. IEEE Access **10**, 82434–82455 (2022)
10. Di Tizio, G., et al.: Software updates strategies: a quantitative evaluation against advanced persistent threats. IEEE TSE **49**(3), 1359–1373 (2023)
11. Fensel, D., et al.: Knowledge Graphs. Springer, Cham (2020). https://doi.org/10.1007/978-3-030-37439-6
12. Fraser, G., et al.: Does automated unit test generation really help software testers? A controlled empirical study. ACM TOSEM **24**(4), 1–49 (2015)
13. Gao, X., et al.: A survey of graph edit distance. Pattern Anal. Appl. **13**, 113–129 (2010)
14. Grzesik, A., et al.: On tripartite common graphs. Combin. Probab. Comput. **31**(5), 907–923 (2022)
15. Ho, G., et al.: Hopper: modeling and detecting lateral movement. In: USENIX Security (2021)
16. IACD: Integrated Adaptive Cyber Defense (IACD) Playbooks (2017)
17. Kaiser, F.K., et al.: Attack hypotheses generation based on threat intelligence knowledge graph. IEEE TDSC (2023)
18. Kryukov, R., et al.: Mapping the security events to the MITRE ATT & CK attack patterns to forecast attack propagation. In: ADIoT Workshop (2022)
19. McLachlan, G.J.: Mahalanobis distance. Resonance **4**(6), 20–26 (1999)
20. Milani Fard, A., et al.: Leveraging existing tests in automated test generation for web applications. In: ACM/IEEE ASE (2014)
21. Navarro, J., et al.: A systematic survey on multi-step attack detection. Comput. Secur. **76**, 214–249 (2018)
22. Nour, B., et al.: A survey on threat hunting in enterprise networks. IEEE COMST (2023)

23. Ontañón, S.: An overview of distance and similarity functions for structured data. Artif. Intell. Rev. **53**(7), 5309–5351 (2020)
24. Puzis, R., et al.: ATHAFI: Agile Threat Hunting And Forensic Investigation. arXiv preprint (2020)
25. Qamar, S., et al.: Data-driven analytics for cyber-threat intelligence and information sharing. Comput. Secur. **67**, 35–58 (2017)
26. Schlette, D., et al.: Do you play it by the books? A study on incident response playbooks and influencing factors. In: IEEE S&P (2023)
27. Team, G.C.A.: Threat Horizons - April 2023 Threat Horizons Report (2023)
28. Tomita, T., et al.: Template-based Monte-Carlo test generation for simulink models. In: CyPhy Workshop (2019)
29. Xia, P., et al.: Learning similarity with cosine similarity ensemble. Inf. Sci. **307**, 39–52 (2015)
30. Yujian, L., et al.: A normalized Levenshtein distance metric. IEEE TPAMI **29**(6), 1091–1095 (2007)

Trade-Off Between Authentication Performance and Detection Time for Zero-Effort Attack in Location-Based Authentication

Ryosuke Kobayashi$^{(\boxtimes)}$ (iD) and Rie Shigetomi Yamaguchi (iD)

The University of Tokyo, 7-3-1 Hongo, Bunkyo-ku, Tokyo, Japan
kobayashi@yamagula.ic.i.u-tokyo.ac.jp

Abstract. In recent years, research on behavioral authentication has been increasing. Behavioral authentication is believed to be suitable for continuous authentication, which can detect changes in the user of a device after logging into a service. However, many previous studies have not addressed how long it takes for an authentication system to detect this change after the user has switched. Therefore, in this paper, we conducted experiments to measure the time it takes for an authentication system to detect imposters while varying the parameters of the authentication system known as the "Time Window". Additionally, within the same experiment, we also evaluated the authentication performance using the True Acceptance Rate (TAR) as the evaluation metric. The results revealed a trade-off relationship between detection time and authentication performance. The experiment used data of 100 individuals randomly selected from approximately 57,000 individuals.

Keywords: Behavioral Authentication · Continuous Authentication · Location · Detection Time · Time Window

1 Introduction

In recent years, there has been a significant increase in research on user authentication methods that utilize behavioral information such as location history. Conventional methods of user authentication rely on information like possession, memorization, and physical characteristics, collectively known as the three factors of authentication [1]. In contrast to these conventional authentication methods, some researchers refer to authentication techniques that utilize behavioral history information as the fourth factor of authentication [2,3]. One of the factors contributing to the recent interest in behavioral authentication is the development of the Internet of Things (IoT). Advancements in sensor technology have enabled highly accurate collection of human behavior data in real-time, which can easily be gathered as electronic information. Particularly, smartphones are equipped with a variety of sensors, allowing for the automatic collection of various types of humans' behavioral data simply by carrying the device. Behavioral authentication techniques utilize the collected behavioral information.

M. Mosbah et al. (Eds.): FPS 2023, LNCS 14552, pp. 70–81, 2024.
https://doi.org/10.1007/978-3-031-57540-2_6

One of the advantages of using IoT technology for behavioral authentication is that it does not require explicit actions from the users during authentication. In methods like password-based authentication, users need to input the information using a keyboard or a touch pad, whereas in biometric authentication methods like fingerprint authentication, users need to provide their biometric information to the sensor. In behavioral authentication, users do not need to consciously input authentication information since sensors can automatically collect user behavior data and the data is inputted to the authentication system. Therefore, behavioral authentication is gaining attention as a convenient method that reduces the burden on users.

Taking advantage of this benefit, behavioral authentication methods are also expected to be used as *Continuous Authentication*. Continuous authentication is a technique that verifies whether the user operating the device after an initial authentication remains the legitimate user and has not changed to someone else [4]. However, using authentication methods that require explicit user input, like passwords, for continuous authentication can be burdensome for users as they need to input information repeatedly [5]. Therefore, employing authentication methods like behavioral authentication that do not require conscious input can enable the detection of changes in the user after login without imposing a significant burden on users.

Behavioral authentication allows for the detection of malicious users who may join a service partway through. However, there is limited research addressing how much of the service usage by malicious individuals can be detected. Existing research on behavioral authentication has primarily evaluated using metrics such as False Acceptance Rate (FAR) and False Rejection Rate (FRR), similar to conventional authentication methods. Among these, Gonzalez-Manzano et al. have proposed a metric called *Detection Time* emphasizing the importance of evaluating the period it takes for the system to detect a malicious user replacing a legitimate user [6]. This paper aims to use this metric to investigate the detection time in behavioral authentication methods using location data. Additionally, it is known that the duration of behavior used for authentication, referred to as the time window, can affect authentication performance in behavioral authentication [7]. This paper also aims to examine how the time window impacts not only authentication performance but also the detection time.

1.1 Classification of Behavioral Authentication

There are various types of behavior utilized for user authentication. Abuhamad et al. [8] categorized the modalities utilized for behavioral authentication and classified them into two types. One is behavioral biometrics utilizing keystroke dynamics, touch gestures, voice, motions, and so on. Another is user profiling which utilizes behavioral profiles, app preference, geolocation-based information, and so on. We focus on location-based authentication in this research, which is included in user profiling.

1.2   Attack for Behavioral Authentication

Rayani et al. [9] introduced some existing researches on behavioral authentication and attack methods for them. They introduced both behavioral biometrics and user profiling regarding behavioral authentication methods. However, they only presented attack methods related to behavioral biometrics such as gait [10], touchscreen [11], keystroke [12], and so on. This implies the absence of research on attack methods for user profiling. Therefore, we focused on attacks against location-based authentication in this study.

1.3   Structure of Paper

The rest of the paper is organized as follows. In Sect. 2, we provide a brief explanation of the key terms that are crucial in this paper, namely, *Time Window* and *Detection Time*. Section 3 describes the authentication method employed in this study, which utilizes location data. Following that, Sect. 4 presents the experimental methodology and its results, and in Sect. 5, we provide an overall summary.

2   Time Window and Detection Time

In this section, we will provide a detailed explanation of the terms *Time Window* and *Detection Time* as mentioned in Sect. 1.

2.1   Time Window

The time window refers to the temporal duration of the information used for authentication. In conventional authentication methods, such as those using passwords or fingerprints, users are unlikely to be conscious of the time window. On the other hand, behavioral information often cannot adequately represent a person's authenticity with just information from a instantaneous moment. To capture individual characteristics, a certain period of behavioral history is required, such as a period from leaving home, walking to the station, taking the train, and to going to work. This length of history is utilized in authentication as the information that represents a person's authenticity. We call this length of history as *Time Window* in this paper.

2.2   Detection Time

The detection time refers to the period it takes for the system to detect an attacker, as proposed by Gonzalez-Manzano et al., from the moment the attacker initiates an attack in continuous authentication. In this section, we will provide a brief explanation of continuous authentication and then proceed to explain the detection time.

Gonzalez-Manzano's Proposal. Gonzalez-Manzano et al. used two metrics, the First Interval of False Positives (FIFP) and First Interval True Negatives (FITN), to explain *Detection Time* in their paper [6]. FIFP represents the duration until the first detection of an attacker, with smaller values indicating a lower likelihood of success for the attacker. FITN, on the other hand, represents the duration required to detect an attacker, limited by a given threshold (TH). From the definitions of these metrics, it is evident that Gonzalez-Manzano et al. argued that a certain period is required by the authentication system from the first detection of an attacker until it correctly identifies them as an attacker. Gonzalez-Manzano et al. used these metrics to define *Detection Time* (*DT*) as follows.

$$DT = \alpha \times (FIFP + TH). \tag{1}$$

Note that α represents the data collection interval.

3   Location-Based Authentication Method

In this section, we will explain the authentication method employed in this paper, which utilizes location data. While there have been numerous proposals for authentication methods using location data in previous research [13,14], this study adopts our proposed location-based authentication method. In this paper, we refer to the location where a user u is present at a specific time t as location information, denoted as $L_u(t) = l$. When the user u and the time t are determined, the location l is uniquely determined as well.

3.1   Characteristics of Behavioral Authentication

Before describing the authentication method, we will explain the characteristics of behavioral authentication. In this paper, behavioral authentication refers to a method that utilizes the habitual patterns of human behavior, particularly focusing on repetitive patterns in daily life activities. Human daily activities exhibit rhythmic patterns on a daily basis. People typically follow a basic activity pattern consisting of daytime activities and nighttime sleep, and these activities become patterned behaviors. While human behavior is patterned, it doesn't mean that the same actions are performed at the exact same times every day. Human behavior patterns exhibit fluctuations, and even if similar patterns of behavior are repeated daily, there may be time lags in their activities. Therefore, to use information from daily life activities for authentication by pattern recognition, it is necessary to implement processing for these fluctuations.

There are fluctuations in both time and location aspects. To leverage the repetition of daily activities for behavioral authentication, it is necessary to implement processing that ignore these fluctuations.

3.2   Overview

Authentication techniques typically consist of two phases which are the enrollment phase and the verification phase, and behavioral authentication follows this

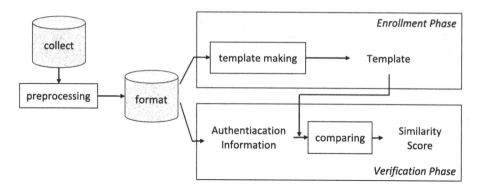

Fig. 1. Overview of Location-based Authentication Method

structure as well. Figure 1 illustrates an overview of the authentication method that utilizes location information. Location data collected undergoes preprocessing and format conversion. In the enrollment phase, template making processes are applied to the formatted data to create a template. In the verification phase, the formatted data is used as authentication information, and a similarity score is calculated by comparing it with the template. If the calculated similarity score is greater than a predefined threshold, authentication is accepted, otherwise, it is rejected.

3.3 Process

In this section, we will provide detailed explanations of the three data processing steps mentioned in the previous section.

Preprocessing. As mentioned in Sect. 3.1, there are fluctuations in behavioral habits. To utilize the repetitiveness of these habits for authentication, it is necessary to implement processing that can ignore these fluctuations. In the context of behavioral authentication, data preprocessing is applied to the collected data to eliminate these fluctuations and transform the data format. The following sections will explain the data transformation processes performed for fluctuations in both time and location.

– Time Fluctuation
  In this method, we attempt to eliminate the time fluctuation by rounding location information for one hour. In other words, at a timestamp $t = (d, time)$ (where d represents the day and $time$ represents the time in hours, minutes, and seconds) and for each hour interval n o'clock $\leq time < (n + 1)$ o'clock $(n = 0, 1, \cdots, 23)$, we process the location information $L_u(d, time)$ as constant. The value to be set is the location where the user stayed the longest during the time interval n o'clock $\leq time < (n + 1)$ o'clock.

– Location Fluctuation

   In this method, we adopt a quadkey [16] as a representation of location to disregard the location fluctuation. Various sizes are defined in the quadkey system, and we adopted 15 level size with sides of approximately 1.2 km each for this research. Throughout this paper, we'll use "l" as the parameter representing the quadkey. In other words, for a given time interval n o'clock $\leq time < (n+1)$ o'clock, if the user spent the longest time in a particular quadkey and designated it as "l," then $L_u(d, time) = l$ (n o'clock $\leq time < (n+1)$ o'clock).

Template Making. A template is information that represents the authenticity of an individual and is created in the enrollment phase based on behavior data collected over a certain period. In this paper, we refer to this period as the template making period. To create a template, it is necessary to assign weights to possible behaviors based on the behavior during the template making period. For example, even if someone consistently commutes to work at the same time every morning, there can be variations in the specific destinations such as commuting to the main office or visiting a client directly. If a user commutes to the client's office once a week and the rest of the time to the main office, treating these two cases with equal certainty would not accurately represent the user's authenticity. Therefore, it is essential to assign weights to possible behaviors. In other words, it is necessary to assign a larger weight to locations frequently stayed and a smaller weight to locations stayed less frequently during the template making period. The template $T_u(h)$ for user u can be obtained using the algorithm shown in Algorithm 1. The process from line 6 to 13 involves assigning weights to each location stayed during the template making period, and from line 14 to 16, the assigned weights are normalized.

Comparing. By comparing the preprocessed behavioral data with the template created in the enrollment phase, a value is calculated. This value is referred to as the "similarity score". Additionally, the information used for authentication by comparing it with the template is called "authentication information", and the period included in the authentication information is referred to as the time window. In other words, the similarity score can be obtained by comparing the authentication information with the template. The similarity score represents the similarity between the authentication information and the template, and the higher the similarity, the higher the score. When we denote the similarity score for user u at d-day h-hour as $S_u(d, h)$, this value is calculated using the algorithm shown in Algorithm 2. The process from line 5 to 7 checks whether the locations included in the authentication information are also present in the template, and if they exist, then it adds the weight of those locations in the template to the similarity score. The similarity score is calculated as an hourly value, as per the formula, and it reflects the result of rounding the behavioral information to hourly intervals after applying the process for behavior fluctuation both in time and location aspects.

Algorithm 1. Template Making Algorithm

Require: Location data
1: D : Template making period
2: $L_u(d, h)$: Location information for user u at d-day h-hour
Ensure: $T_u(h)$ Template
3: **function** MAKE_LOCTEMPLATE($D, L_u(d, h)$)
4:     $T_u(h) \leftarrow \{\}$
5:     $c \leftarrow 0$
6:     **for** d in D **do**
7:         **if** $L_u(d, h)$ in $T_u(h)$ **then**
8:             $T_u(h)[L_u(d, h)] += 1$
9:         **else**
10:            $T_u(h)[L_u(d, h)] \leftarrow 1$
11:        **end if**
12:        $c += 1$
13:    **end for**
14:    **for** t_{loc} in $T_u(h)$ **do**
15:        $T_u(h)[t_{loc}] \leftarrow T_u(h)[t_{loc}]/ c$
16:    **end for**
17:    **return** $T_u(h)$
18: **end function**

Algorithm 2. Similarity Score Calculation Algorithm

Require: Location data
1: $L_u(d, h)$: Location information for user u at d-day h-hour
2: $T_u(h)$: Template for user u at h-hour
Ensure: $S_u(d, h)$ Similarity score
3: **function** COMPARE_LOC($L_u(d, h)$, $T_u(h)$)
4:     $S_u(d, h) \leftarrow 0$
5:     **if** $L_u(d, h)$ in $T_u(h)$ **then**
6:         $S_u(d, h) \leftarrow T_u(h)[L_u(d, h)]$
7:     **end if**
8:     **return** $S_u(d, h)$
9: **end function**

3.4 Verification

From the similarity scores calculated in Sect. 3.3, it is verified whether authentication is accepted or not. It is necessary to set a threshold value k in advance for the verification. With the predefined k, the verification is conducted as follows.

$$\begin{cases} if\ S_u(d, h)\ \geq\ k & then \quad accept \\ else & reject \end{cases}$$

4 Experiment

In this section, we will explain the experiments conducted in this research.

4.1 Dataset

In this experiment, we utilized MITHRA dataset [15]. The MITHRA project gathered data from approximately 57,000 participants with location information collected from 16,027 individuals by their installing MITHRA apps to their own smartphones. From this dataset, we randomly selected 100 participants who were *Android* users and had participated in the project for 60 days or more to use as the data for this experiment. We used the data from the first 60 days for the selected 100 participants in this experiment. Among these 60 days, we designated the first 30 days as the template making period and the remaining 30 days as the data for the test period in which we compared with the template.

4.2 Experimental Scenario

In this research, we conducted two experiments. The first one focused on examining authentication performance when varying the time window. The second one focused on examining the detection time under similar variations in time window. The time window was set for 1 h, 2 h, 3 h, 4 h, 6 h, 8 h, 12 h, and 24 h, respectively. For evaluating authentication performance, this experiment employed TAR (True Acceptance Rate) as the assessment metric. TAR is defined as follows.

$$TAR = \frac{\# \ acceptance}{\# \ authentication \ test}.$$

Note that the term $\#$ *authentication test* represents the number of authentication tests conducted, while $\#$ *acceptance* indicates the count of accepted authentication within these tests. The number of authentication attempts varies depending on the *Time Window* value (TW), and given that the test period is 720 h (30 days), the number of authentication tests was calculated as ($720 \div TW$) times.

We used DT as the metrics for the detection time, which was explained in Sect. 2.2. In this experiment, TH was set to 1, and α was set to 1 h. To calculate DT, it is necessary to set up an attacker, and the details of the attack scenario will be described below.

Attack Scenario. The attacker's goal is to impersonate a legitimate user, and the attacker performs a zero-effort attack to achieve this goal. In the context of this experiment on the location-based authentication, a zero-effort attack means that the attacker acquires a legitimate user's smartphone at a certain point. Subsequently, the attacker continues with his/her usual behavior while possessing the device, attempting to impersonate a legitimate user. It is important to note that the attacker is assumed to be unaware of the legitimate user's behavioral patterns.

The dataset used in this experiment does not include data where the attacker has acquired a legitimate user's device. It was simulated that the two individuals exchanged devices at a certain location where they have stayed and then continued with their usual behavior. After the device exchange, authentication is performed by comparing the template of the legitimate user with the authentication information of the attacker.

In this dataset, there were 170 cases that met these conditions. For each case, the transition of similarity scores after the assumed device exchange was calculated. The similarity scores after exchange were calculated by using the function $COMPARE\_LOC(L_a(d, h),\ T_u(h))$ in Algorithm 2 with the legitimate user denoted as u and the attacker as a. The detection time was determined by finding the time it took for the similarity score to fall below the threshold of $k = 0.1$ as set in this experiment.

4.3   Experimental Result

In this section, we will describe the experimental results.

Authentication Performance. Figure 2 is a box plot representing the distribution of TAR (True Acceptance Rate) for the 100 users across different TW. The horizontal axis represents the TW, and the vertical axis represents TAR. As a general trend, it can be observed that TAR increases as the TW becomes longer. Additionally, the minimum values are significantly lower than the median values for all TW. This indicates that while the authentication method used in this study achieves a high level of accuracy for many users, it may not perform as well for a minority of users. Specifically, focusing on the results for TW of 24 h, the majority of users (67 out of 100) achieved a TAR of 1.0, indicating high accuracy. However, the user with the lowest TAR in this group could only achieve a TAR of 0.67.

Detection Time. Figure 3 illustrates the progression of average similarity scores for each TW in the 170 cases targeted in this simulation. The horizontal axis represents the time elapsed since the device swap of two individuals, while the vertical axis indicates the similarity scores. The detection time refers to the time when the similarity score falls below the threshold. If we apply the definition of Gonzalez-Manzano et al., $\alpha = 1\,h$ and $TH = 1$ in Eq. (1). It is evident from this figure that a longer time window result in longer detection time. Specific DTs are provided in Table 1.

Looking at Table 1, it can be seen that the DT is 0 for TW of 1 and 2 h. This means that authentication had already failed before the device was swapped. As seen in Fig. 2, it is evident that authentication is successful for many cases even with TW of 1 and 2 h. However, in the 170 cases targeted in this data, the average similarity score did not exceed the threshold. Especially, when TW was

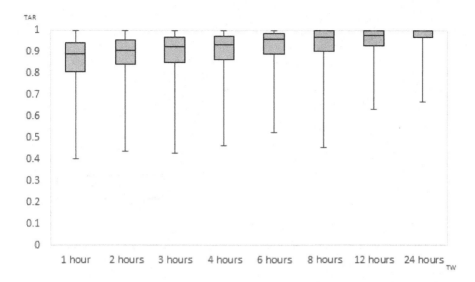

Fig. 2. The distribution of TAR across Time Windows for 100 users

Table 1. Detection time for each Time Window

Time Window (TW) (hour)	1	2	3	4	6	8	12	24
Detection Time (DT) (hour)	0	0	1	2	3	4	7	17

set to 1 h, the average similarity score before the device swap was 0, indicating that not a single case out of the 170 succeeded in authentication.

4.4 Discussion

In this experiment, we examined the changes in authentication accuracy and detection time when varying TW. As a result, we found that increasing TW leads to higher authentication accuracy, but at the same time, it results in longer DT. In this evaluation, we have used TAR to measure authentication performance. A high TAR indicates that users are correctly authenticated, implying high convenience and minimal stress for the users. On the other hand, longer DT mean that when a user's device such as a smartphone is stolen, there is a higher likelihood of unauthorized use of that device. This situation could potentially lead to higher risks for users. From the results of this experiment, we can conclude that there is a trade-off relationship between authentication performance and detection time, where improving one aspect tends to negatively affect the other.

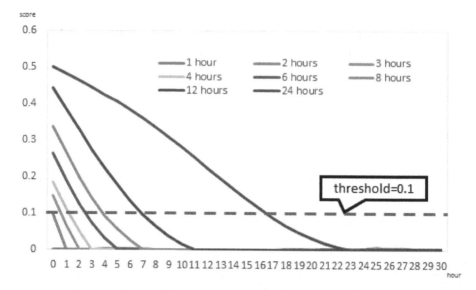

Fig. 3. The evolution of similarity scores for each Time Window after a zero-effort attack

5   Conclusion

In this paper, we have explained the characteristics of behavioral authentication and emphasized its potential for enabling continuous authentication without burdening users. The advancement of IoT technology in recent years has made it easier to collect behavioral information, contributing to research in the field of behavioral authentication. However, despite the expectation that behavioral authentication will be used for continuous authentication, there has been limited research on how quickly attacks can be detected when users are compromised. Therefore, we have pointed out the lack of research in this area. To address this gap, we have described an authentication method using location information, one type of behavioral data. We have conducted experiments to verify how changes in the time window affect authentication accuracy and how detection times change when an attack is assumed to occur due to a stolen device. The results of our verification have revealed a trade-off relationship between authentication accuracy and detection time. This suggests that there is no one-size-fits-all time window, and the appropriate value should be determined based on the specific application in which authentication is used.

In this study, we focused on an authentication method that utilizes location information. However, there are many other proposed methods in the field of behavioral authentication. It will be important to calculate detection times for these alternative methods as well. Additionally, while we only considered one attack scenario in this study, it is necessary to explore other attack scenarios as well. These are challenges that need to be addressed in future research.

References

1. Grassi, P., Garcia, M., Fenton, J.: Digital Identity Guidelines. NIST Special Publication (SP) 800-63-3 (2020)
2. Yamaguchi, R.S., Nakata, T., Kobayashi, R.: Redefine and organize, 4th authentication factor, behavior. Int. J. Network. Comput. **10**(2), 189–199 (2020)
3. Choi, S., Zage, D.: Addressing insider threat using "where you are" as fourth factor authentication. In: 2012 IEEE International Carnahan Conference on Security Technology (ICCST), pp. 147–153. IEEE (2012)
4. Dasgupta, D., Roy, A., Nag, A.: Advances in User Authentication. Springer, Cham (2017). https://doi.org/10.1007/978-3-319-58808-7
5. Traore, I.: Continuous Authentication Using Biometrics: Data, Models, and Metrics. IGI Global (2011)
6. Gonzalez-Manzano, L., Mahbub, U., de Fuentes, J.M., Chellappa, R.: Impact of injection attacks on sensor-based continuous authentication for smartphones. Comput. Commun. **163**(1), 150–161 (2020)
7. Kobayashi, R., Yamaguchi, R.S.: Behavioral authentication method utilizing wi-fi history information captured by IoT device. In: 2017 International Workshop on Secure Internet of Things (SIoT), pp. 20–29. IEEE (2017)
8. Abuhamad, M., Abusnaina, A., Nyang, D., Mohaisen, D.: Sensor-based continuous authentication of smartphones' users using behavioral biometrics: a contemporary survey. IEEE Internet Things J. **8**(1), 65–84 (2020)
9. Rayani, P.K., Changder, S.: Continuous user authentication on smartphone via behavioral biometrics: a survey. Multimedia Tools Appl. **82**(2), 1633–1667 (2023)
10. Kumar, R., Phoha, V.V., Jain, A.: Treadmill attack on gait-based authentication systems. In: 2015 IEEE 7th International Conference on Biometrics Theory, Applications and Systems (BTAS), pp. 1–7. IEEE (2015)
11. Khan, H., Hengartner, U., Vogel, D.: Targeted mimicry attacks on touch input based implicit authentication schemes. In: Proceedings of the 14th Annual International Conference on Mobile Systems, Applications, and Services, pp. 387–398 (2016)
12. Khan, H., Hengartner, U., Vogel, D.: Augmented reality-based mimicry attacks on behaviour-based smartphone authentication. In: Proceedings of the 16th Annual International Conference on Mobile Systems, Applications, and Services, pp. 41–53 (2016)
13. Mahbub, U., Chellappa, R.: PATH: person authentication using trace histories. In: 2016 IEEE 7th Annual Ubiquitous Computing, Electronics & Mobile Communication Conference (UEMCON), pp. 1–8. IEEE (2016)
14. Sieranoja, S., Kinnunen, T., Fränti, P.: GPS trajectory biometrics: from where you were to how you move. In: Robles-Kelly, A., Loog, M., Biggio, B., Escolano, F., Wilson, R. (eds.) S+SSPR 2016. LNCS, vol. 10029, pp. 450–460. Springer, Cham (2016). https://doi.org/10.1007/978-3-319-49055-7_40
15. Kobayashi, R., Saji, N., Shigeta, N., Yamaguchi, R.S.: Large scale PoC experiment with 57,000 people to accumulate patterns for lifestyle authentication. In: Proceedings of the Ninth ACM Conference on Data and Application Security and Privacy, pp. 161–163 (2019)
16. Microsoft: Bing Maps Tile System. https://learn.microsoft.com/en-us/bingmaps/articles/bing-maps-tile-system. Accessed 15 Sept 2023

SADIS: Real-Time Sound-Based Anomaly Detection for Industrial Systems

Awaleh Houssein Meraneh$^{(\boxtimes)}$, Fabien Autrel, Hélène Le Bouder,
and Marc-Oliver Pahl

IMT Atlantique, IRISA, Rennes, France
{awaleh.houssein-meraneh,fabien.autrel,helene.le-bouder,
marc-oliver.pahl}@imt-atlantique.fr

Abstract. Industrial cyber-physical systems are critical infrastructures vulnerable to cyber-attacks. Anomaly and intrusion detection are widely used approaches to enhance the security of these systems. This paper investigates side-channel leakages, particularly sound, for high-accuracy detection of intrusions and anomalies in various industrial systems. Despite sound signal's advantages, such as low-cost equipment, minimal computational requirements, and non-invasive measurement. Current sound-based anomaly detection (SAD) methods face challenges such as sensitivity to background noise, unbalanced sound data, computational costs, and detection accuracy. To tackle these issues, we introduce robot-arm sound dataset (RASD) and present a real-time sound-based anomaly detection for industrial systems (SADIS) approach that uses a simple and efficient method to fingerprint expected sound data with reduced dimensions. Our experiments demonstrate that the SADIS approach achieves an average attack detection rate of over 96%, with a detection time of less than 1 s and low computational costs.

Keywords: Industrial systems · anomaly detection · side-channel leakage · sound · Autoencoder · Mahalanobis distance · real-time

1 Introduction

industrial cyber-physical systems (ICPS) face increased vulnerability to cyber-physical attacks due to growing interconnectivity between physical and cyber systems [8]. Attacks on these systems can cause collateral damage, as illustrated by the Stuxnet cyberattack [6], emphasizing the need for robust security, including anomaly and intrusion detection. Anomaly and intrusion detection systems (IDS) are security measures for detecting unexpected behavior, with current struggles in accurately identifying deviations in ICPS's physical system leading to delayed responses and false alarms that risk the manufacturing process. This paper investigates the use of side-channel leakages, particularly sound, for high-accuracy detection of intrusions and anomalies in various industrial systems. Therefore, sound-based anomaly detection (SAD) method proves to be practical

© The Author(s), under exclusive license to Springer Nature Switzerland AG 2024
M. Mosbah et al. (Eds.): FPS 2023, LNCS 14552, pp. 82–92, 2024.
https://doi.org/10.1007/978-3-031-57540-2_7

and widely applicable in domains such as public video surveillance, speech analysis and recognition, healthcare, predictive maintenance of industrial. To our knowledge, it has not yet been applied to detect cyber-physical attacks.

Existing SAD methods face challenges such as sensitivity to background noise, unbalanced sound data and domain shift challenges. Addressing these issues is crucial for enhancing detection performance and adaptability across diverse environments [7]. While many SAD methods [3,12,13] are performed offline, few studies [1,2,10] perform real-time detection providing early anomaly detection. This work compares the SADIS approach to existing methods, evaluating side-channel leakage, real-time performance, parameter sensitivity, robustness against noise, and overall effectiveness in detecting cyber-physical attacks (Table 1). This paper introduces a real-time SADIS approach for detecting cyber-physical attacks in ICPS. It addresses the challenges of existing methods, including computational costs, detection accuracy, and noise robustness. The SADIS approach efficiently extracts relevant features from sound data using dimension reduction via time-average spectrum (TAS) or principal component analysis (PCA). Additionally, the SADIS employs an autoencoder (AE) for data classification and utilizes the Mahalanobis distance (MD) as an anomaly-scoring function, enhancing detection performance. Moreover, the main contributions of this work are twofold. First, we have generated a sound dataset, robot arm sound dataset (RASD), to address unbalanced sound data challenges[1]. Secondly, we have developed the SADIS approach, assessing its robustness using the RASD dataset and enhancing its adaptability through validation on diverse industrial systems.

Table 1. Comparison of related works in anomaly detection for industrial systems. The '−' symbol indicates that the research question was not addressed in the study, while the ✓ symbol indicates that the study investigated the research question

Articles	Side-channel leakage	Real-time performance	Parameter sensitivity	Robustness against noise	Comparison with existing approach
Baseline [3]	sound	-	-	-	-
IDNN [12]	sound	-	-	-	✓
Pu et al. [10]	power	✓	✓	-	-
U-net [13]	sound	-	-	-	✓
Bayram et al. [2]	sound	✓	-	✓	✓
Bai et al. [1]	power	✓	-	✓	✓
SADIS	**sound**	✓	✓	✓	✓

The paper is structured as follows: Sect. 2 presents the SADIS approach, Sect. 3 details the experimentation setup and results evaluation, and Sect. 4 concludes with the strengths and limitations of the SADIS approach.

---

[1] https://github.com/a23houss/sadis_experimentation_code.

2   The SADIS Approach

2.1   Overview of SADIS Appraoch

As depicted in Fig. 1, SADIS is trained on normal sound data using unsupervised learning during the training phase. The training sound data are preprocessed using the Eqs. (4), (5), (6) defined in Sect. 2.2. Then, the preprocessed sound data are fitted to the autoencoder model, which learns relevant features and minimizes reconstruction error using the following Eq. (1):

$$\mathcal{L}(x, \hat{x}) = \frac{1}{n} \sum ||x - \hat{x}||^2; \tag{1}$$

Commonly, the reconstruction error (mean squared error (MSE)), denoted as e (Eq. (1)), compute the difference between input x with reconstruction $\hat{x}$. The distribution of normal reconstruction errors sets the threshold for anomaly detection by using Eqs. (2).

$$MD(e, \Delta) = \sqrt{(e - \mu_\Delta)^T V_\Delta^{-1} (x - \mu_\Delta)}. \tag{2}$$

The MD is computed with Eq. (2), where e is an observation vector, μ_Δ and V_Δ^{-1} are respectively mean value and inverse covariance matrix of a distribution. The SADIS approach efficiently detects anomalies using MD as a scoring function. In online detection 2.4, incoming sound data is preprocessed and compared to the threshold to classify it as abnormal or normal. SADIS is unique in its feature-extracting preprocessing, autoencoder's efficiency, and accurate anomaly scoring for raw sound signals regardless of duration.

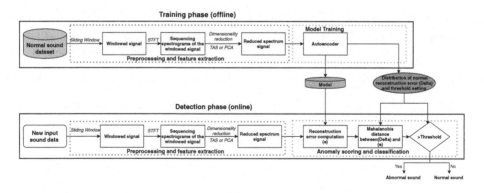

Fig. 1. Overview of the proposed real-time SADIS approach

2.2   Preprocessing Step

The sound dataset, denoted by X, comprises N audio signals represented by raw audio signals x_i:

$$X = \{x_1, x_2, \ldots, x_N\}. \tag{3}$$

Each audio signal x_i is composed of n time series samples. In anomaly detection, preprocessing involves dimensionality reduction and feature extraction to enhance classification algorithms' performance and efficiency. In this paper, a sliding window method is used during the initial data preprocessing phase to detect deviant points by capturing sequential dependencies.

Sliding Window. After applying the sliding window algorithm to each audio signal $x_i \in X$, it can be represented as:

$$SW(x_i) = W = \{w_1, \ldots, w_l\}; \tag{4}$$

where $w_j = [j \cdot (k - t), (j + 1) \cdot (k - t) + t]$ contains k samples of the raw signal, k corresponds to the window length, and t is the overlap size between windows. The value of l depends on the time window-length k and its overlap t and is such that $l < n$. This paper explores the impact of window length on the performance of the SADIS approach in terms of detection rate and time.

Feature Extraction. The audio signal is divided into overlapping windows, and the STFT is computed for each window to extract its spectrogram. This results in a sequence of spectrograms, each represented by a two-dimensional array of size $m \times n^*$, where m represents frequency components and n^* represents the number of features. Thus, the windowed audio signal W can be represented as a sequence of spectrograms given by:

$$STFT(W) = \{s_1, \ldots, s_l\}; \tag{5}$$

where s_j is the spectrogram obtained from the j-th window. The windowed signal W has a total size of $l \cdot (m, n^*)$, where l represents the number of windows.

Reduction of Dimensions. To enhance SAD in industrial systems and reduce dimensions and noise, SADIS employs either time-average spectrum (TAS) or principal component analysis (PCA) as dimensionality reduction techniques.

Time-Average spectrum (TAS) computes the average of each spectrogram [9] along the spectrogram matrix's m-dimension, to minimize machine operation noise, as shown by the equation:.

$$s_j^{TAS} = \frac{1}{m} \sum_{i=1}^{m} s_{i,j}. \tag{6}$$

Here, $s_{i,j}$ corresponds to each spectrogram of the windowed signal, and s_j^{TAS} is the resulting time-averaged spectrogram, which is a vector of size n^*. By applying the TAS method for each spectrogram of the windowed signal W, we concatenate all the averaged spectrograms into a matrix of dimension (l, n^*) represented by: $S^{TAS} = [s_1^{TAS}, s_2^{TAS}, \ldots, s_l^{TAS}]$.

Principal component analysis PCA identifies the principal components of the dataset by finding eigenvectors of its covariance matrix and projects the data onto a lower-dimensional space. PCA reduces each windowed signal's spectrogram s_j into a smaller vector denoted as s^{PCA}. By applying PCA to each spectrogram in the windowed signal, we obtain the following matrix: $S^{PCA} = [s_1^{PCA}, s_2^{PCA}, \ldots, s_l^{PCA}]$. The resulting signal S^{PCA} is a matrix of dimension (l, n^*), similar to the TAS reduction method described earlier.

The preprocessed signal, denoted as S, results from windowing, spectrogram extraction, and dimensionality reduction (TAS or PCA). We assess their impact on detection rate and time by varying window length and reduction methods. Through experiments, we demonstrate the significance of preprocessing methods in obtaining input data with reduced dimensions capturing relevant features.

2.3   Offline Training Phase

SADIS is trained with only normal sound data during the training phase due to its unsupervised learning. The training sound data are preprocessed using the predefined equations in Sect. 2.2. The autoencoder is trained and learns latency and relevancy features of training data while minimising the reconstruction error by using the MSE function defined in Eq. (1). Let S_i denotes the i-th input signal data, while $\hat{S}_i$ signifies the i-th reconstructed signal data generated by the autoencoder The computed reconstruction errors e during training are defined as follows:

$$e_i = MSE(S_i, \hat{S}_i). \tag{7}$$

From these errors e_i, we define a distribution Δ of normal reconstruction error as $\Delta = [e_0, \cdots, e_{n_{tr}}]$, where n_{tr} denotes the size of training data. The defined distribution of normal reconstruction errors Δ sets the threshold and scores anomalies by using the Mahalanobis distance (MD) defined in Eq. (2).

Thresholding. The study addresses the challenge of setting a threshold (σ) for anomaly detection due to the variability and complexity of anomalies. The trained autoencoder reconstructs a protion of normal sound data, yielding a set of reconstruction errors (E^σ). Using the Mahalanobis distance (MD) and a precomputed distribution (Δ), SADIS calculates distance values (D^σ). Multiple threshold evaluations lead to using the Gamma distribution percentile. Following the DCASE challenge baseline [3], this approach fits a gamma distribution to D^σ scores and uses the inverse of the 90th percentile of the cumulative distribution function as the decision threshold (σ). After offline training, the model, the distribution of normal reconstruction errors (Δ), and the threshold (σ) are saved.

2.4   Online Detection Phase

New sound data x^{new} is preprocessed using the equations from Sect. 2.2. The resulting preprocessed sound data S^{new} is given as input to the trained model. Its reconstruction error e^{new} is computed as the mean squared error (MSE) between S^{test} and the reconstructed data ($\hat{S}^{new}$). Additionally, the distance metric (MD) between e^{new} and the previously computed distribution Δ is calculated using Eq. (2). If this distance value surpasses the threshold σ, the new sound data is classified as abnormal; otherwise, it is considered normal.

3   The SADIS Experimentation and Results

3.1   Dataset

We conduct experiments on one sound public dataset malfunctioning industrial machine investigation and inspection (MIMII) and our collected sound dataset from a robot arm called RASD.

MIMII Dataset. The MIMII dataset [11] is widely used in SAD research for identifying malfunctions in industrial machinery. It consists of recordings from four machine types (valves, pumps, fans, and slide rails). Each 10-second recording contains both operational machine sounds and ambient noise, serving as a benchmark to assess our approach and compare it with existing methods.

Robot Arm Sound Dataset (RASD): Our Sound Dataset. We established an experimental platform using the *TinkerKit Braccio* and *Arduino Uno* to evaluate our methodology, creating a diverse dataset of industrial robotic arm sounds. The robot arm, mirroring real-industrial production, has six axes controlled by servo motors[2] This dataset stands out for its authentic attack vectors and reproducibility. Details of our setup and the sound dataset are provided in the following paragraphs.

Normal Behavior of RASD. The robot arm, executing precise movements from point A to point B, generates normal sound data during typical manufacturing operations. This data accurately represents the expected sound profile of a functioning robot arm in real-world settings.

Anomalous Sound Generation and Vectors. Creating anomalous sound data is challenging due to the rarity of abnormal patterns in real-life scenarios [2]. To address this, attack vectors from literature, focusing on speed and trajectory angle modifications [5], are employed to simulate abnormal behavior in the robot arm. Speed modification attacks, similar to those in Stuxnet [6], can be challenging to detect as they mimic normal behavior. Different anomaly vectors, such as *Anomaly Vector 1* (slight speed increase), *Anomaly Vector 2* (higher acceleration with material risks), and *Anomaly Vector 3* (speed increase across all axes with significant risks), are used to generate abnormal sounds, representing primary types of attacks in the context of robotic arms.

---

[2] For more details: https://store.arduino.cc/products/tinkerkit-braccio-robot.

3.2   Evaluation Criteria

ROC Curve Analysis. The receiver operator characteristic (ROC) curve evaluates binary classification performance by plotting true positive rate (TPR) against false positive rate (FPR), with a higher AUC indicating improved differentiation between normal and abnormal data within models [4].

Real-Time Detection Time. In real-time anomaly detection, detection time (detection time (DT)) is crucial. Computed according to Sect. 2.4, DT is the sum of execution times for preprocessing time (PT), model time (MT), and the computation of error reconstruction and Mahalanobis distance (t_{score}), expressed as:

$$DT = PT + MT + t_{score}. \tag{8}$$

Efficient real-time anomaly detection prioritizes minimizing detection time.

3.3   Results: The SADIS Detection Performance

The SADIS Evaluation on MIMII Dataset. This experiment compares the SADIS approach with existing SAD methods, presented in Sect. 1, using the MIMII dataset. The results show the average detection rate of TAS and PCA reduction techniques, measured by AUC values. Table 2 provides a summary of the comparison. Prior preliminary tests are conducted to select an optimal window length for the MIMII dataset.

Table 2. The SADIS evaluation on MIMII dataset (AUC values (%)

Machine Type	Baseline [3]	Unet [13]	IDNN [12]	SADIS
Fan	66	80	71	**92**
Pump	73	**85**	75	**77**
Slider	85	90	90	**91**
Valve	66	84	**90**	85

The results of this experiment show that the SADIS approach outperforms existing methods in two machine types (fan and slider) and is comparable in the remaining two. These results indicate its potential for anomaly detection across various industrial systems. These findings also highlight the adaptability of the SADIS approach to different conditions and equipment used for sound data collection.

Robustness of the SADIS Approach. In both offline training and testing, we conduct experiments using RASD to assess the SADIS approach's robustness to parameter sensitivity and noises. RASD has a longer time length compared to MIMII, with 10 s for MIMII and 23 s for RASD. This preliminary experiment aims to analyze the impact of window-length variation and noise factors. By varying the window length and introducing background noise, we evaluate their effects on the SADIS approach's detection rate, time, and overall robustness against background noise.

Parameters Sensitivity and Selection. Parameter sensitivity analysis is conducted to assess the impact of different parameters on the detection rate and time performance of the approach. Experimental results are summarized in Table 3 and Table 4. Table 3 and Table 4 outline the performance results and detection time results of SADIS approach using TAS and PCA reduction method respectively.

Table 3. parameter sensitivity results of SADIS using TAS as reduction method

Window length (s)	Performance AUC (%)	Time Taken		
		DT(s)	PT(s)	MT(s)
0.2	91	3.54	3.1	0.43
0.25	94	**0.97**	**0.95**	**0.01**
0.5	95	5.14	4.33	0.8
0.75	**96**	4.12	3.5	0.61
1	94	5.14	4.81	0.67
1.25	95	5.27	4.65	0.62

Table 4. parameter sensitivity results of SADIS using PCA as reduction method

Window length (s)	Performance AUC (%)	Time Taken		
		DT(s)	PT(s)	MT(s)
0.2	92	**1.06**	**1.05**	**0.01**
0.25	92.5	1.34	1.21	0.13
0.5	93	6.86	6.24	0.62
0.75	95	8.71	8.05	0.65
1	96	4.41	4.24	0.17
1.25	**97**	6.75	6.53	0.22

Results show minimal impact of varying window length on SADIS-TAS and SADIS-PCA detection rates (AUC values), maintaining an average TPR of 99% and FPR of 2%. However, it significantly influences detection time (DT), while t_{score} remains negligible. PT strongly affects DT, as shown in the result Table 3 and Table 4, with an average MT of 0.4 s. For the RASD dataset, TAS and PCA use window lengths of 0.25 s and 0.2 s, respectively; different datasets may require varying window lengths.

Robustness of SADIS Against Background Noise. We assess SADIS's sensitivity to background noise using synthetic test data with varying noise levels

(0.1 to 0.5). These experiments provide valuable insights, considering the known sensitivity of sound parameters to noise in industrial environments. For instance, a noise factor of 0.1 indicates low background noise, while 0.5 represents higher noise levels. The results of this analysis are presented in Table 5 and Table 6.

Table 5. SADIS-TAS detection performance with noise factor

Noise factor	AUC (%)	DT (s)
0.1	71.6	0.42
0.2	70.8	0.42
0.3	69.2	0.42
0.4	67.0	0.41
0.5	58.0	0.42

Table 6. SADIS-PCA detection performance with noise factor

Noise factor	AUC (%)	DT (s)
0.1	82.5	0.48
0.2	82.2	0.49
0.3	81.8	0.48
0.4	81.5	0.49
0.5	81.0	0.49

PCA is less affected by background noise compared to TAS, although it has a longer computation time. These results partially address the domain shift challenge discussed in the introduction section, as the presence of background noise represents a target domain (test data) different from the source domain (train data).

Real-time SADIS Performance Under Different Anomalies Vectors. The real-time performance of the SADIS approach is evaluated in this section, with results presented in Table 7. Three anomaly vectors are generated and described in Sect. 3.1. These experiments assess SADIS's applicability in real-world scenarios, detecting anomalies with background noise and domain shift conditions.

Table 7. Real-time SADIS performance under different anomalies vectors

Anomaly vector	SADIS-TAS				SADIS-PCA			
	FPR(%)	TPR(%)	AUC(%)	DT (s)	FPR(%)	TPR(%)	AUC(%)	DT (s)
1	1.2	98.4	95	1.86	2.5	95	91	1.4
2	1	97	94	2.15	3	92	85	1.35
3	**0.02**	**99.8**	**99.9**	1.90	**0**	**100**	**100**	**0.92**

SADIS proves highly effective in the results, particularly excelling at detecting anomaly vector 3, considered the most dangerous, with a 100% detection rate for PCA and 99.9% for TAS. Notably, SADIS achieves an impressively low detection time of 1.90 s for TAS and 0.92 s for PCA. While anomaly vector 2 performs slightly below vector 3, it still outperforms anomaly vector 1. Despite the close similarity of anomaly vectors 1 and 2 to nominal behavior, SADIS detects anomalies with an average rate of 92% and an average time of 1.7 s. This underscores SADIS's capability to detect even subtle deviations, addressing domain shift challenges and successfully identifying anomalies in the presence background noise and other factors.

4 Conclusion

In this paper, we introduced RASD and presented SADIS, a real-time sound-based anomaly detection approach for industrial systems. With a detection rate exceeding 96% and an average detection time of less than 1 s, SADIS effectively identifies anomalies, even those with subtle deviations. The SADIS approach is compatible with various industrial systems, as demonstrated by its high detection rate on the MIMII dataset. Moreover, the method exhibits reduced sensitivity to background noise. Despite its promising real-time performance, efforts should focus on minimizing human intervention for handling the low false positive rate below 1%. Future research could explore leveraging multiple parameters to enhance side-channel fingerprinting robustness for improved anomaly detection.

Acknowledgments. This research is part of the chair CyberCNI.fr with support of the FEDER development fund of the Brittany region.

References

1. Bai, Y., Park, J., Tehranipoor, M., Forte, D.: Real-time instruction-level verification of remote IoT/CPS devices via side channels. Disc. Internet of Things **2**, 1 (2022)
2. Bayram, B., Duman, T.B., Ince, G.: Real time detection of acoustic anomalies in industrial processes using sequential autoencoders. Expert Syst. **38**, 12564 (2021)
3. Koizumi, Y., et al.: Description and discussion on dcase2020 challenge task2: Unsupervised anomalous sound detection for machine condition monitoring. arXiv preprint arXiv:2006.05822 (2020)
4. Kumar, R., Indrayan, A.: Receiver operating characteristic (ROC) curve for medical researchers. Indian Pediatr. **48**, 277–287 (2011)
5. Maggi, F., Quarta, D., Pogliani, M., Polino, M., Zanchettin, A.M., Zanero, S.: Rogue robots: Testing the limits of an industrial robot's security. Technical report, Trend Micro, Politecnico di Milano (2017)
6. Matrosov, A., Rodionov, E., Harley, D., Malcho, J.: Stuxnet under the microscope. ESET LLC, September 2010
7. Mnasri, Z., Rovetta, S., Masulli, F.: Anomalous sound event detection: a survey of machine learning based methods and applications. Multimed. Tools App. **81**, 5537–5586 (2021)
8. Novak, T., Gerstinger, A.: Safety-and security-critical services in building automation and control systems. IEEE Trans. Ind. Electron. **57**, 3614–3621 (2009)
9. Park, Y., Yun, I.D.: Fast adaptive RNN encoder-decoder for anomaly detection in SMD assembly machine. Sensors **18**, 3573 (2018)

10. Pu, H., He, L., Zhao, C., Yau, D.K., Cheng, P., Chen, J.: Detecting replay attacks against industrial robots via power fingerprinting. In: Conference on Embedded Networked Sensor Systems (2020)
11. Purohit, H., et al.: MIMII dataset: sound dataset for malfunctioning industrial machine investigation and inspection. arXiv preprint arXiv:1909.09347 (2019)
12. Suefusa, K., Nishida, T., Purohit, H., Tanabe, R., Endo, T., Kawaguchi, Y.: Anomalous sound detection based on interpolation deep neural network. In: 2020 IEEE ICASSP (2020)
13. Van Truong, H., Hieu, N.C., Giao, P.N., Phong, N.X.: Unsupervised detection of anomalous sound for machine condition monitoring using fully connected u-net. J. ICT Res. App. **15**, 1–15 (2021)

A Resilience Component for a Digital Twin

Valeria Valdés[1]([✉])[iD], Fatiha Zaidi[2][iD], Ana Rosa Cavalli[1,3][iD],
and Wissam Mallouli[1][iD]

[1] Montimage EURL, Paris, France
{valeria.valdes,wissam.mallouli}@montimage.com
[2] Université Paris-Saclay, CNRS, ENS Paris-Saclay, Laboratoire Méthodes Formelles,
91190 Gif-sur-Yvette, France
fatiha.zaidi@universite-paris-saclay.fr
[3] Institut Politechnique, Telecom SudParis, Paris, France

Abstract. Industry 4.0 has popularized Cyber-Physical Systems (CPSs), engineered systems integrating physical components with computerized controls for process management. Despite efforts by academia and industry to address CPSs challenges, security remains a key concern. This involves identifying vulnerabilities, weaknesses, and threats. The primary objectives of security are the evaluation of CPSs' security status, uncovering flaws, and suggesting risk mitigation. Nevertheless, besides lists of several CPSs security improvement techniques and methodologies for detecting CPSs security issues, little emphasis is paid to their resolution. This paper analyzes existing techniques to enhance resilience in CPSs, encompassing both design and operational phases to mitigate identified risks. Additionally, we introduce the integration of a resilience component into a Digital Twin (DT) framework. This component utilizes the capabilities of the DT to oversee resilience mechanisms within the system, monitor system activity, and respond effectively to security events.

Keywords: Cyber Physical Systems · Resilience · Digital Twin · Security · Mitigation

1 Introduction

Cyber Physical Systems (CPSs) refers to systems where the physical components are interconnected through communication technologies to create efficient control systems [18]. Comprising physical and cyber layers, CPSs use sensors to collect data, controllers manage system behavior. The cyber layer, a network of connected components, facilitates message transmission for tasks like controller configuration. This integration supports coordination in complex systems, enabling constant monitoring, control, and adaptation of CPSs.

This work is partially supported by the European Union's Horizon Europe research and innovation program under grant agreement No 101070455 (DYNABIC).

CPSs find applications in domains like smart grids, transportation, healthcare, smart cities, and homes [5]. However, they face heightened security risks due to their critical roles. Resilience, defined as the ability to resist, absorb, recover or adapt to adversity or a changing conditions [7], plays a crucial role in CPSs. This involves proactive and reactive measures. While cyber security and resilience share overlapping concepts, resilience is primarily concerned with ensuring the continuity of system operations during adverse conditions or disruptions. In this context cyber security is closely related, focusing on protecting and defending systems against cyber attacks [19].

A Digital Twin (DT) is a virtual replica of a system, widely used in CPSs and networks [21]. DTs incorporate real-time data from the physical system, enabling bidirectional data exchange [16] and enhancing CPS resilience through real-time adaptation. Despite their potential to enhance CPS resilience, challenges remain in scalability, performance, and system impact. Scalability involves managing larger systems efficiently, while performance may be affected by changes, potentially causing cascading effects. The DT's simulation capability allows comprehensive analysis before implementing changes, reducing risks and consequences.

The main contribution of this paper is described as below:

- Introduction of a novel resilience component tailored for Digital Twin technology, enhancing its capability to effectively respond to security events in CPSs. This component serves as a critical addition to improve resilience of CPSs.
- Integration of the resilience component developed within a DT architecture. This integration showcases the adaptability of our approach, allowing existing DT systems to easily incorporate security measures.
- Experimental validation using a model of a Electrical Vehicle Charging Station, allowing the resilience component to monitor and react to flood attacks against the central system of the architecture using a moving target defense approach.

The remainder of this paper is organized as follows. Section 2 presents the related work. Section 3 presents various resilience mechanisms and techniques. Section 4 presents the proposal of a DT extension with a resilience component. Section 5 presents the application and evaluation. The discussion is presented in Sect. 6, and final remarks and conclusions in Sect. 7.

2   Related Work

DTs are an emerging and powerful tool for understanding and controlling complex systems, researchers are applying them in different domains and research about them has increased since its first proposed approach in 2006 by Hellen Gil [14]. This section provides an overview of recent research studies that focus on enhancing resilience in CPSs by leveraging the capabilities of DTs and the use of alternative methodologies and strategies.

The academic community extensively explores methodologies for securing and enhancing resilience in CPSs, particularly in smart grids and power systems [13,20,22]. Studies address security controls, attack detection, resilience in industrial CPSs [8] and proposing resilience frameworks [4]. However, none of these studies consider the use of DT to enhance CPS resilience.

Various studies delve into the utilization of DTs for enhancing resilience in CPSs.. Brucherseifer *et al.* [3] propose a DT framework covering analysis, optimization, and automated low-level decisions. Becue *et al.* [2] view DTs as tools for root cause analysis. Saad *et al.* [15] employ IoT-based energy CPSs to detect attacked components through agent consensus. Lektauers *et al.* [12] utilize DTs for simulation and data sharing. Faleiro *et al.* [9] focus on healthcare DT applications, discussing security layers. Hussaini *et al.* [11] propose a DT defense mechanisms taxonomy, introducing a Secured DT Development Life Cycle based on layer architecture.

The research studies reviewed highlight the role of DT in enhancing CPS resilience. However, a common limitation is absence of specific strategies for incident response due to the need for event and domain specific approaches.

Resilience metrics quantify a system's vulnerability and offer a comprehensive understanding of its response to diverse challenges and changes. They aid in understanding system behavior during events, enabling post-event analysis and evaluating resilience strategies. Various studies discuss and define generic resilience metrics. Haque *et al.* [10] consider asset criticality, risk, and network topology, while Colibianchi *et al.* [6] include path redundancy, device status, and quality of service. Barbeau *et al.* [1] introduces two novel control-theoretic concepts, k-steerability and l-monitorability for determining CPS resilience. Segovia *et al.* [17] propose a resilience metric for a single system variable extended to an overall stability metric assessing attack impact across the entire system. These metrics quantify post-event resilience. In a real-time data-driven context like a DT, the performance metric stands out for real-time monitoring, comparing model and actual data in the DT interface. When an attack is detected, and the system fully recovers its desired performance, an analysis can measure resilience, utilizing factors such as absorb and recovery time as mentioned in previous studies.

3   Resilience Mechanisms and Techniques

3.1   Proactive Techniques

Proactive mechanisms are strategies applied before detecting an attack or unusual events, enhancing system resilience by design. Intrusion Detection Systems (IDS) monitor CPSs using policies, historical data, and attack signatures. Advanced monitoring integrates machine learning for early detection, optimizing models and reconstructing data. Proactive strategies include risk assessment to identify critical CPS components and allocate resources for protection.

Diversification techniques are proactive strategies that hide specific segments of the system to disrupt the adversary understanding and dynamically alter the attack surface. Redundancy is a form of diversity, it involves creating varied versions of the same component, reducing vulnerability attacks focused on specific weaknesses. In this context, Moving Target Defense (MTD) seamlessly switch to alternative components with different designs. Moreover, diversification techniques also include the dynamic change of components positions, resources, and pathways. These constant adjustments decrease system predictability, establishing a barrier that requires adversaries to invest more resources and time to deduce the internal behavior of the system.

Isolation and segmentation are techniques employed in the design of CPSs. Isolation creates separate environments for independent components, preventing an adversary with control of one component from accessing others. Even if the components are independent, being in the same environment makes it easier for an adversary to get access from one to the another. Similarly, segmentation divides the CPS into components or subsystems that interact with each other. The goal is to limit the adversary from getting access from one component to another.

To achieve resilience by design, several classical guidelines can be followed, such as the use of secure communication protocols, authentication control, user privilege restrictions, secure software usage, firewalls, and security best practices to ensure confidentiality, integrity, and availability.

3.2   Reactive Techniques

Reactive mechanisms respond to detected unusual events, aiming to restore normal CPS operation and functionality. As part of reactive techniques, adaptive response dynamically alters the system's behavior and configuration upon event detection to mitigate damage, maintain the system operations and integrity. It employs strategies like incident response plans, where the system selects a specific defense strategy based on the characteristics of the detected event. CPSs may adopt dynamic code changes to reduce their attack surface. However, debugging challenges can arise due to the nature of the code.

Once an incident is detected and addressed, it's crucial to analyze the event to identify the vulnerability that led to its occurrence. Post-event analysis provides insights into the root cause, allowing long-term actions for preventing similar events in the future and improving CPS resilience and security.

To prevent similar events in other CPSs, the use of incident sharing platforms facilitate the exchange of security information, threat, attack details, and security techniques among multiple CPSs, promoting collective defense against potential security events, though sharing sensitive data requires careful consideration. This collaborative approach serves as a collective defense to protect CPSs and mitigate potential security events.

As CPS face a variety of attack types, relying solely on a single defense technique often proves inadequate to protect the system. Given that certain defense techniques are attack-specific, it is a common practice to employ a multilayered defense to elevate the overall security and resilience of CPS. Combining security by design with reactive mechanisms enhances the system's adaptability to various attacks, ensuring comprehensive protection against a broad spectrum of security events.

4   Resilience Component

This research proposes integrating a built-in resilient component into a DT architecture, managing both existing and new resilience mechanisms within the system. The resilience component takes advantage of the DT's feedback capability to control resilience mechanisms in the system. Since the DT allows to collect information of a system in real time and collect information from a model, such as a predictive models, these two sources of information can be compared to obtain real-time resilience metrics representing the current state of the system that can be visualized and monitored through the DT.

As outlined in Sect. 3, resilience mechanisms fall into proactive or reactive categories. Proactive mechanisms run continuously, with their execution controllable by the resilience component. Reactive mechanisms, respond to specific events, triggered by the resilience component when necessary, updating DT models is essential whenever system changes occur.

The reactive mechanism workflow is illustrated in Fig. 1, involves the resilience component responding to event detection by taking appropriate actions and updating the system model. Proactive mechanisms follow a similar workflow, where the resilience component continuously updates the system and model without relying on event detection.

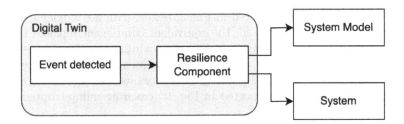

Fig. 1. Workflow of the Resilience Component for reactive mechanisms

As an example of a resilience mechanism, the resilience component employs Moving Target Defense (MTD). To implement MTD, it is necessary to have beforehand a set of equivalents components for the same functionality, exhibiting the same behavior but with different implementations, making them less vulnerable to the same attacks. The resilience component instruct the system to replace a component with an equivalent one, and updates the system model accordingly.

In addition to the MTD mechanism, the resilience component has the capability to integrate various other mechanisms, both existing within the system and newly introduced ones. This integration aims to leverage the strengths of theses mechanisms to enhance system resilience. For new mechanisms, they can be implemented as new services within the resilience component. As for the existing mechanisms, the resilience component can manage and control them by establishing connections or utilizing available APIs. This allows the resilience component to effectively oversee and enhance the system's resilience by leveraging the capabilities of these integrated mechanisms.

5   Application of Resilience Component in a DT

MADT4B[1] (Multi-Aspect DT for Business Continuity) is an ongoing real-time DT platform that provides system insights. It connects and synchronizes a CPS in real time, offering contextual information and extending DT capabilities for business continuity. It uses a Knowledge Graph (KG) to represent system and features a NeoDash dashboard linked to a Neo4j database backend.

The resilience component is integrated as a new service to the DT's backend, including resilience mechanisms. Functioning centrally, the resilience component controls these mechanisms. Management is through the DT's GUI, with a new "Mechanism" node in the KG meta-model. The MTD mechanism replaces a vulnerable asset with an equivalent, which refers to a new component that provides identical services as the original but with a distinct implementation.

To maintain isolation between the original component and its equivalents, the connection between them is present only in the knowledge graph presented by the DT, indicating their equivalence. However, these connections do not exist in the physical system itself. It is responsibility of the MTD mechanism to rearrange the connections once a component is replaced with its equivalent.

The MTD mechanism, depicted in Fig. 2, begins with a component denoted as S in Fig. 2a. Represented as S', the equivalent component replaces the original one. S_a represent the component or set providing functionality, while S_x represents those required for S to operate. Subsequently, connection are duplicated to ensure service availability in Fig. 2b. After establishing connections, the old component is safely disconnected in Fig. 2c, ensuring uninterrupted service during the transition.

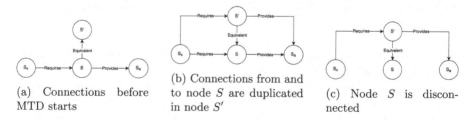

(a) Connections before MTD starts

(b) Connections from and to node S are duplicated in node S'

(c) Node S is disconnected

Fig. 2. Simple MTD replacement

For component replacement, we initially opt for random selection. However, a prioritization strategy based on factors such as component status, performance metrics, costs, and other criteria can enhance the selection process for optimal system replacement.

---

[1] https://github.com/SINTEF-9012/madt-neodash.

5.1 Modeled System

The resilience component is tested using an electric vehicle charging station (EVCS) scenario, representing a CPS. The EVCS includes physical components like charging stations and virtual components, such as the charging station management system (CSMS). Multiple charging stations (CS) are connected to a network switch for Ethernet connectivity to the CSMS. The CSMS, hosted on a private cloud, remotely maintains and monitors the CSs using the Open Charge Point Protocol (OCPP) over the Internet. A router and WiFi access points enhance Internet connectivity. For grid-related protection, a Feeder Protection Relay (FPR) is synchronized with a GPS clock. Figure 3 depicts the high-level architecture.

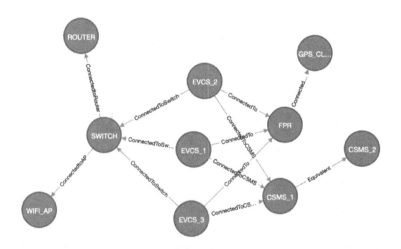

Fig. 3. Knowledge Graph for EVCS

5.2 Adversary Model: Flood Attack to CSMS, Detection and Reaction

We considered a Heartbeat flood attack from a CS to the CSMS, aiming to saturate the communication channel and CSMS resources. The Heartbeat message serves the purpose of indicating that a charging point is currently connected and operational. The initial entry point of the adversary is the charging point. The adversary can gain control over this component of the system using various spoofing techniques, including eavesdropping on communication or executing man-in-the-middle attacks. Additionally, the adversary could steal identification details from the charging point device, such as TLS certificates to gain access.

The resilience component, monitoring the CSMS logs, as depicted in Fig. 4a, includes a monitor system fetching connection details from the KG. This system connects to the InfluxDB database, focusing on Heartbeat logs for rule-based flood attack detection.

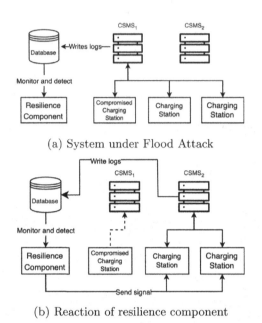

(a) System under Flood Attack

(b) Reaction of resilience component

Fig. 4. Detection and reaction of flood attack to CSMS

Under normal conditions, heartbeat messages are sent every 8 min, but during flooding attack, the frequency increases to about 0.1 s. The detection system uses a tolerance attribute for rule-based detection.

Upon detecting an attack, the affected CS is flagged in the DT's KG, triggering a MTD strategy as depicted in Fig. 4b. Two CSMS implementations were used: a python application[2] with the ocpp library, and a second extension[3].

We conducted 10 flooding attacks, messages were randomly sent from a charging station at intervals d seconds, $d \in (0, 1]$. Table 1 compares system behavior with and without the resilience component. The system, with the resilience component, showed a lower average response time during attacks. Recovery is not recorded without the resilience component since a single charging station's attack isn't sufficient to bring down the system. However, with the resilience component, recovery is considered as the transition time in one charging station when switching to a new CSMS. In both scenarios, the services remains available, resulting in no downtime. Figure 5 displays logs in the resilience component and one charging station when an event is detected, and MTD is triggered.

---

[2] https://github.com/mobilityhouse/ocpp.
[3] https://github.com/villekr/ocpp-asgi.

Table 1. System behaviour without resilience component and with it.

Metric	Without resilience component	With resilience component
Response time	0.47 [s]	0.38 [s]
Recover time	-	0.005 [s]
Downtime	0 [s]	0 [s]

2023-09-15 11:55:53,221 DT: Live monitoring started for asset EVCS_1, with tolerance 0.5 and window size 5.0
INFO: 172.18.0.1:60218 - "POST /monitor/start HTTP/1.1" 200 OK
2023-09-15 11:56:18,367 DT: Event detected for asset EVCS_1 at 2023-09-15 11:56:18.355412
2023-09-15 11:56:18,371 DT: Sending change request to EVCS_2
2023-09-15 11:56:18,371 DT: Sending change request to EVCS_3

(a) Log in resilience component, send an update to charging stations.

INFO:ocpp:EVCS_2: receive message [2,"b43defbc-3830-4976-bd52-ed3b9b98e212","BootNotification",{"chargingStation":{"model":"ResilienceComponent","vendorNam
e":"ResilienceComponent"},"reason":"Unknown","customData":{"vendorId":"RC","newIp":"192.168.66.14","newPort":9000}}]
Received csms update notification at 2023-09-15 11:56:18,474
Connection restablished with new server 192.168.66.14 at 2023-09-15 11:56:18,681

(b) Log in charging station upon receiving update and reconnect to the new CSMS.

Fig. 5. Logs when an event is detected and MTD is triggered

6   Discussion

DTs provide diverse services to CPSs, and security is a crucial aspect. Despites its capabilities in real-time information collection, the MADT4BC DT platform lacks an inherent resilience component. The bidirectional communication allows the DT to detect anomalies, while a resilience component offers protection and feedback for mitigation.

To assess the resilience component's response effectiveness, several aspects should be considered. This includes scalability in terms of the number of adversaries and the system's complexity. It is important to test the system in complex and realistic scenarios for ensure its reliability, evaluate its performance in both normal conditions as well as during attacks. For MTD, when replacing components with equivalents, connected elements need reestablishment. If the equivalent has existing connections, no need for this step. In hybrid cases, renew remaining connections for seamless integration. Moreover, for subscription services, updating all subscribers is vital. This informs them of changes and allows adjustments to their setup and interactions.

Additionally, when selecting a resilience mechanism, it's crucial to weigh the cost of implementation and execution within the system. Some mechanisms might promise better performance but implementations costs can be significant. In such cases, lower performance options that meet systems constraints could be necessary.

Lastly, the goal is to achieve self-healing systems that autonomously recover from attacks and security events. However, the operator involvement in the feedback loop remains vital. The DT can suggest responses based on event complexity. For common security scenarios, the DT can trigger automatic responses, forming a hybrid resilient component. This balances automated and manual strengths, ensuring effective response to diverse incidents. MTD empowers self-healing, removing the need for manual operator responses.

7   Conclusion

In this study, we presented the integration of a resilience component into the DT architecture, aiming to improve resilience in a critical infrastructure by responding to detected events in the CPS. The response of the component varies according on the nature of the event. Our focus was on implementing a reactive MTD mechanism within the resilience component, requiring the implementation of equivalent components with identical functionality beforehand. To facilitate the MTD implementation while preserving the generic DT meta-model architecture, an additional attribute indicating the current status of a component is added to the DT. This attribute enables differentiation between healthy and attacked components following incident detection. Furthermore, this attribute also denotes whether the component is active in the system, enabling the MTD to trigger a component switch using an equivalent counterpart.

As part of our future work, we intend to delve into further research on reactive strategies. This exploration aims to enable the resilience component to prioritize among these strategies and provide the most appropriate response for events based on relevant metrics.

References

1. Barbeau, M., Cuppens, F., Cuppens, N., Dagnas, R., Garcia-Alfaro, J.: Metrics to enhance the resilience of cyber-physical systems. In: 2020 IEEE 19th International Conference on Trust, Security and Privacy in Computing and Communications (TrustCom), pp. 1167–1172 (2020). https://doi.org/10.1109/TrustCom50675.2020.00156
2. Bécue, A., Maia, E., Feeken, L., Borchers, P., Praça, I.: A new concept of digital twin supporting optimization and resilience of factories of the future. Appl. Sci. **10**(13), 4482 (2020). https://doi.org/10.3390/app10134482, https://www.mdpi.com/2076-3417/10/13/4482
3. Brucherseifer, E., Winter, H., Mentges, A., Mühlhäuser, M., Hellmann, M.: Digital twin conceptual framework for improving critical infrastructure resilience. at - Automatisierungstechnik **69**(12), 1062–1080 (2021). https://doi.org/10.1515/auto-2021-0104
4. Cassottana, B., Roomi, M.M., Mashima, D., Sansavini, G.: Resilience analysis of cyber-physical systems: a review of models and methods. Risk Anal. (2023). https://doi.org/10.1111/risa.14089
5. Chen, H.: Applications of cyber-physical system: a literature review. J. Ind. Integr. Manage. **02**(03), 1750012 (2017). https://doi.org/10.1142/S2424862217500129
6. Colabianchi, S., Costantino, F., Di Gravio, G., Nonino, F., Patriarca, R.: Discussing resilience in the context of cyber physical systems. Comput. Ind. Eng. **160**, 107534 (2021). https://doi.org/10.1016/j.cie.2021.107534
7. Committee, D.R.S., et al.: DHS risk lexicon. Department of Homeland Security. Technical report (2008)

8. Ding, D., Han, Q.L., Xiang, Y., Ge, X., Zhang, X.M.: A survey on security control and attack detection for industrial cyber-physical systems. Neurocomputing **275**, 1674–1683 (2018). https://doi.org/10.1016/j.neucom.2017.10.009

9. Faleiro, R., Pan, L., Pokhrel, S.R., Doss, R.: Digital twin for cybersecurity: towards enhancing cyber resilience. In: Xiang, W., Han, F., Phan, T.K. (eds.) BROAD-NETS 2021. LNICST, vol. 413, pp. 57–76. Springer, Cham (2022). https://doi.org/10.1007/978-3-030-93479-8_4

10. Haque, M.A., Shetty, S., Krishnappa, B.: Cyber-Physical Systems Resilience: Frameworks, Metrics, Complexities, Challenges, and Future Directions, Chapter 12 (2019)

11. Hussaini, A., Qian, C., Liao, W., Yu, W.: A taxonomy of security and defense mechanisms in digital twins-based cyber-physical systems. In: 2022 IEEE International Conferences on Internet of Things (iThings) and IEEE Green Computing and Communications (GreenCom) and IEEE Cyber, Physical and Social Computing (CPSCom) and IEEE Smart Data (SmartData) and IEEE Congress on Cybermatics (Cybermatics), pp. 597–604 (2022). https://doi.org/10.1109/iThings-GreenCom-CPSCom-SmartData-Cybermatics55523.2022.00112

12. Lektauers, A., Pecerska, J., Bolsakovs, V., Romanovs, A., Grabis, J., Teilans, A.: A multi-model approach for simulation-based digital twin in resilient services. WSEAS Trans. Syst. Control. **16**, 133–145 (2021). https://doi.org/10.37394/23203.2021.16.10

13. Paul, S., Ding, F., Utkarsh, K., Liu, W., O'Malley, M.J., Barnett, J.: On vulnerability and resilience of cyber-physical power systems: a review. IEEE Syst. J. **16**(2), 2367–2378 (2022). https://doi.org/10.1109/JSYST.2021.3123904

14. Pivoto, D.G., de Almeida, L.F., da Rosa Righi, R., Rodrigues, J.J., Lugli, A.B., Alberti, A.M.: Cyber-physical systems architectures for industrial internet of things applications in industry 4.0: a literature review. J. Manuf. Syst. **58**, 176–192 (2021). https://doi.org/10.1016/j.jmsy.2020.11.017, https://www.sciencedirect.com/science/article/pii/S0278612520302119

15. Saad, A., Faddel, S., Youssef, T., Mohammed, O.A.: On the implementation of IoT-based digital twin for networked microgrids resiliency against cyber attacks. IEEE Trans. Smart Grid **11**(6), 5138–5150 (2020). https://doi.org/10.1109/TSG.2020.3000958

16. Segovia, M., Garcia-Alfaro, J.: Design, modeling and implementation of digital twins. Sensors **22**(14), 5396 (2022). https://doi.org/10.3390/s22145396, https://www.mdpi.com/1424-8220/22/14/5396

17. Segovia, M., Rubio-Hernan, J., Cavalli, A.R., Garcia-Alfaro, J.: Cyber-resilience evaluation of cyber-physical systems. In: 2020 IEEE 19th International Symposium on Network Computing and Applications (NCA), pp. 1–8 (2020). https://doi.org/10.1109/NCA51143.2020.9306741

18. Segovia., M., Rubio-Hernan., J., Cavalli., A.R., Garcia-Alfaro., J.: Switched-based control testbed to assure cyber-physical resilience by design. In: Proceedings of the 19th International Conference on Security and Cryptography - SECRYPT, pp. 681–686. INSTICC, SciTePress (2022). https://doi.org/10.5220/0011327300003283

19. of Standards, N.I., Technology: Guide for conducting risk assessments. Technical report (2012). https://doi.org/10.6028/nist.sp.800-30r1

20. Tahar, B.M., Amine, S.M., Hachana, O.: Machine learning-based techniques for false data injection attacks detection in smart grid: a review. In: Hatti, M. (ed.) Advanced Computational Techniques for Renewable Energy Systems. LNNS, vol. 591, pp. 368–376. Springer International Publishing, Cham (2023). https://doi.org/10.1007/978-3-031-21216-1_39

21. Wagg, D., Worden, K., Barthorpe, R., Gardner, P.: Digital twins: state-of-the-art future directions for modelling and simulation in engineering dynamics applications. ASCE-ASME J. Risk Uncertain. Eng. Syst. Part B Mech. Eng. **6**, 030901 (2020). https://doi.org/10.1115/1.4046739
22. Zhang, D., et al.: A comprehensive overview of modeling approaches and optimal control strategies for cyber-physical resilience in power systems. Renew. Energy **189**, 1383–1406 (2022). https://doi.org/10.1016/j.renene.2022.03.096

Author Index

M. Mosbah et al. (Eds.): FPS 2023, LNCS 14552, pp. 105–106, 2024.
https://doi.org/10.1007/978-3-031-57540-2

Printed in the United States
by Baker & Taylor Publisher Services